Advance praise for *Pause and Reset*

"This is truly an evidence-based book written from the perspective of a parent who is also one of the leading scientists in the field. The book is clearly written in lay language and thus is ideal for a parent who is trying to decide whether or not their child has a problem and if so, where to get help."

—**Charles P. O'Brien**, MD, PhD, University of Pennsylvania

"*Pause and Reset* is an acutely needed guide for anyone who interacts with our youth today. Gaming addiction or Internet gaming disorder is fairly new compared with society's other addictions, but is much more critical because it is affecting our children at such an early age as well as their parents. We as parents, clinicians, educators and policymakers need to be able to understand, recognize, assess and address this behavior. Top addiction expert Nancy Petry does an outstanding job of presenting practical, clear, research-based advice which will be an indispensable guide for digital families."

—**Pamela Hurst-Della Pietra**, DO, Founder and President, Children and Screens: Institute of Digital Media and Child Development and Clinical Assistant Professor of Health Care Policy and Management, School of Health Technology and Management, Stony Brook Medicine

PAUSE AND RESET

*A Parent's Guide to Preventing
and Overcoming Problems
with Gaming*

NANCY M. PETRY, PH.D.

OXFORD
UNIVERSITY PRESS

Oxford University Press is a department of the University of Oxford. It furthers the University's objective of excellence in research, scholarship, and education by publishing worldwide. Oxford is a registered trade mark of Oxford University Press in the UK and certain other countries.

Published in the United States of America by Oxford University Press
198 Madison Avenue, New York, NY 10016, United States of America.

© Oxford University Press 2019

Library of Congress Cataloging-in-Publication Data
Names: Petry, Nancy M, author.
Title: Pause and reset : a parent's guide to preventing and overcoming problems with gaming / Nancy M. Petry, Ph.D.
Description: New York, NY : Oxford University Press, 2019. |
Includes bibliographical references and index.
Identifiers: LCCN 2018038824 (print) | LCCN 2018041228 (ebook) |
ISBN 9780190279493 (UPDF) | ISBN 9780190279509 (EPUB) |
ISBN 9780190279486 (pbk. : alk. paper)
Subjects: LCSH: Video game addiction—Prevention. |
Video games and children. | Parenting.
Classification: LCC RC569.5.V53 (ebook) | LCC RC569.5.V53 P47 2019 (print) |
DDC 616.85/84—dc23
LC record available at https://lccn.loc.gov/2018038824

9 8 7 6 5 4 3 2 1

Printed by Webcom, Inc., Canada

Contents

SECTION 2 Intervention

Preface

Kids around the world have been playing video or electronic games for decades. With the advent of the Internet, these games have developed in sophistication and accessibility, becoming very high-tech and varied in nature and content. There are many types of games available, appealing to different age groups, genders, and personalities. Most kids play video games, and many parents condone, or at least allow, occasional playing. However, some parents have strong reservations about overuse of this technology.

Perhaps nowhere are concerns as strong as they are in some Southeast Asian countries. In South Korea and China, for instance, excessive Internet gaming has been likened to an epidemic, which has led to the emergence of specialized "treatment camps" where excessive gaming is treated as an addiction. Excessive and problematic gaming has become a part of the medical and psychiatric vernacular in these countries. In response to these concerns, physicians, psychologists, and other mental health professionals from around the world, including the United States, began lobbying professional societies and governments for official recognition of a psychological condition associated with excessive video gaming.

Nearly 10 years ago, the American Psychiatric Association (APA) began the process of updating its classification system for psychiatric disorders, the *Diagnostic and Statistical Manual of Mental*

Disorders (DSM). This was an important event because this manual guides diagnosis and treatment for mental health conditions not only in the United States but in other countries as well. The updates can impact millions of people and the care they receive.

My research has focused on treating substance use and gambling disorders, so when the APA invited me to join a work group involved in planning the fifth revision of the DSM, I presumed these would be the sections in which I would participate. What I did not expect was that I would be charged with working on Internet gaming disorder. The American Medical Association (AMA) released a report in 2007[1] encouraging the APA to consider gaming addiction or Internet addiction more broadly as a mental disorder. I chaired the APA's subcommittee on non-substance addictions. Through this process, my interests in gaming and Internet addiction grew. I reviewed the scientific literature in these areas and learned about the condition from people with gaming problems and their parents, as well as from experts around the globe who treat people with addictions to gaming.

Throughout this process, I gained a great deal of insight into Internet gaming disorder. This book represents a culmination of my efforts in researching gaming problems and their treatment. Many other clinicians, researchers, and patients contributed to and supported the inclusion of a condition related to gaming in a section of the DSM known as the research appendix, and to the ideas and concepts in this book.

There is still a long way to go in terms of understanding Internet gaming disorder, and I expect that the upcoming years will see major advances in that understanding. The DSM-5 provides guidelines for the classification of this condition, but clearly, we need more research on diagnosis. We also know relatively little about the course of symptoms. Although clinicians are—and should be—treating gaming and Internet use problems, the interventions available to them are typically eclectic and nonspecific. We need to have a better understanding of which treatments lead to improvements above and beyond those that occur naturally.

As you already know if you're reading this book, parents are those most often seeking answers to questions about problematic Internet gaming, such as how to tell if a child has a problem with gaming, and what to do about it. My goal in the following pages is to translate scientific research and clinical practice guidelines into language that (as clearly and comprehensively as possible) answers these questions for parents and other loved ones. They may not be perfect answers, and often they will be works in progress—but I aim to provide you with the best information we have right now. Parents and other loved ones can use the exercises and information in this book without professional assistance, or in conjunction with it. Clinicians can also apply these exercises and techniques when working with patients, or recommend them to parents of their patients.

Throughout the book I provide case examples to depict common themes or issues. In some cases, they represent extremes. In others, they are typical examples. All vignettes in this book represent composites of cases; they are not based on actual people.

Acknowledgments

I thank the many people who have assisted directly and indirectly in the process of writing this book. They include members of the APA Work Group on Substance-Related Disorders who helped me formalize these ideas. Special thanks go to Dr. Charles O'Brien, the Chair of this Work Group, for arguing for recognition of gaming disorder. Appreciation also goes to Dr. Florian Rehbein, who invited me to participate in an international work group on gaming disorder. With them and other collaborators, I've moved my research in a new direction.

I thank Dr. Kristyn Zajac, my colleague at UConn School of Medicine, for providing detailed and valuable comments on a draft of this book. Dr. Zajac, along with Drs. Rocio Chang and Meredith Ginley, have taken on the role of serving as initial therapists for some patients and their families suffering from this condition. I also thank many members of my research staff, both those involved with our gaming studies—Amy Novotny, Julie Urso, and Sean Sierra—and many others who are keeping our other projects going as we embark upon this new area: Drs. Sheila Alessi, Carla Rash and Bill Blakey, Matt Brennan, Sarah Coughlin, Marcia DeSousa, Ruth Fetter, Damaris Hernandez, Trish Lausier, Steve Mackinnon, Betsy Parker, and Wendy Soneson. I thank Andrea Zekus, my editor, for providing excellent suggestions and advice throughout the writing of this book.

I also am grateful for my husband, Dr. William White, and our children, Hannah and Noah. They were toddlers when I began this book and I am watching them grow up in a world where electronic games and online connections are the norm, but they constantly remind me that real-life relationships and activities will always be irreplaceable.

About the Author

Nancy M. Petry, Ph.D., was Professor of Medicine at the University of Connecticut School of Medicine. Her work was funded by the National Institute on Drug Abuse, the National Institute of Mental Health, the National Institute on Alcohol Abuse and Alcoholism, and the Eunice Kennedy Shriver National Institute of Child Health and Human Development. Dr. Petry conducted research on addictive disorders ranging from substance use disorders to internet gaming and gambling disorder.

PAUSE AND RESET

1

Introduction

You come home from work every night to find your teenage son glued to the computer, playing some video game that looks violent and absurd, in your opinion. You know these games are popular, and all the kids seem to be playing them. But are other kids playing them as much as your child? Your son is totally wrapped up in them. He never gets together with friends in person, and he seems to have no other interests. On the other hand, you are glad he is not doing drugs or getting into trouble at school. But can kids develop an addiction to video games the same way they do to drugs? Can addiction to video games get as bad as drug addiction?

Gaming addiction, or Internet gaming disorder, is a condition in which a person develops significant problems related to electronic or video games ("gaming"). If you are reading this book, then you may already know that the people most likely to play electronic games and to experience difficulties with them are adolescents and young adults.

The types of problems that can develop from excessive gaming range from interpersonal (concerning friends or family) to academic (or work-related for those out of school), psychological (depression, suicidality), and physical (e.g., insomnia, seizures). In the most extreme cases, aggressive behaviors, legal difficulties, or even death may result from overuse of games. For example, the media, especially in Southeast Asian countries, have detailed accounts of players dying from excessive long-term playing episodes.[1] Thankfully, such cases are exceedingly rare.

Most often, problems arise with excessive *online* gaming. However, gaming disorder can also occur with *offline* games. People who play games on any electronic device, including computers, televisions, PlayStations, Xboxes, Nintendos, tablets (iPads), and smartphones (e.g., iPhones), can have the condition known as Internet gaming disorder.

Research indicates that the vast majority of children and adolescents in the United States play video games. One nationally representative study of teenagers, for example, found that up to 99% of boys and 94% of girls play electronic games.[2] The average amount of time youth spend gaming is about 12 hours per week,[3] although some play for substantially longer periods. Others, of course, play less.

Excessive gaming can destroy lives, and it has. Extreme cases suggest that some adolescents and young adults have dropped out of high school or college because they spent too much time gaming. Even adults can experience severe adverse consequences. There have been documented cases of game-induced seizures in people who have spent many days playing online.[4] In other instances, parents have neglected their children due to excessive gaming.[5]

These are clearly the most severe types of problems. Although most cases do not rise to these extremes, it's normal for parents to be concerned about their children's behaviors whenever they are in excess. Parents may become worried when their child is neglecting homework to play games, or is staying up all night gaming and is too tired to get up for school the next day. Some parents notice that their child rarely socializes with others and spends all free time on video games. Some children start to cover up how much they are playing. They play at night or secretively, and they lie about how much time they are spending gaming. Many parents understandably wonder if their child is developing an addiction to gaming, and what they can do about it.

Consider the case of Jennifer and Max.

Jennifer is the mother of 12-year-old Max, who seems to be spending all his time playing video games. Jennifer bought her son a Nintendo when he was 8, and she now regrets getting him started so young. It was easier to control his playing when he was younger because she could put the game out of reach. Then, she could allow access only occasionally on school nights and weekends. As Max got older, it became more difficult to restrict his gaming. He began asking for games for his birthday and as Christmas presents. His aunts, uncles, and grandparents were happy to fulfill his requests. Then he started playing games online as well as on the Nintendo, and now Jennifer cannot distinguish his computer use for gaming from computer use for doing schoolwork. She does not feel comfortable taking away his laptop or restricting its use, because he needs it for his homework assignments. When she tries to look over at what he is doing, he quickly shuts the screen or flips to another site. Max's grades have been dropping. He stays up playing through all hours of the night, and he finds it difficult to get out of bed in the mornings. He rarely spends time with friends, unless they are playing video games together. Jennifer is worried that her son is addicted to video games.

This is just one example of how problems can arise from excessive gaming. Some cases are clearly problematic, while others are less obvious. If you are reading this book, you are concerned about your child. You want answers about whether your child's game playing is typical, or if it exceeds the bounds of normal play. You want to know how you can prevent or stop problems from developing or progressing.

This book answers some very important questions related to Internet gaming disorder. It describes scientific thinking about the condition, and outlines the characteristics of those most likely to develop problems with gaming. It also provides guidance about how to prevent it, as well as how to minimize problems that have already developed or seem to be escalating. Although this book and the examples in it are directed toward parents, adults can also experience problems with excessive gaming, and the steps and recommendations are also applicable, with some modifications, to partners or others who care about an adult with a gaming problem.

This book focuses on Internet gaming, because it is one of the most common Internet activities with which individuals develop problems. People use computers and other electronic devices excessively for other purposes as well. These include texting, Internet browsing, social media, shopping, working, and gambling. Many of the suggestions and tips in this book are applicable to other forms of excessive computer and Internet use. However, the emphasis is on gaming because it is a specific online activity that can create great difficulties. It is also the Internet-related activity that has the most consistent scientific evidence related to its harms.

Because Internet use generally—and Internet gaming specifically—is a relatively new phenomenon, the science behind it is just emerging. It is important to remember that the Internet was not commonly available in households until about the year 2000. The types of games that people are playing today have changed dramatically over the past 15 years. In addition, the number of kids playing them excessively has risen markedly. This is the first generation of youth growing up with widespread Internet access. For the vast majority, games are available online 24 hours a day, 365 days a year.

Electronic games, of course, have been in existence since the late 1970s, with the advent of Atari. Video gaming arcades were at the height of their popularity in the 1980s, with these being fashionable venues for teenagers and preteens to hang out. In the late 1980s, the Nintendo Game Boy emerged, and soon after, other handheld video games. Even then parents expressed concerns about video games. Their worries were in many ways similar to those being expressed by parents today, many of whom themselves grew up in the video game arcade era.

A big difference, however, between the older and newer types of games relates to their complexity and ubiquitous availability. Games today encourage the development and maintenance of online relationships. With the original video games, competition existed only among individuals playing on the same machine. In contrast, some of the most popular online games now—including and especially Massively Multiplayer Online Role-Playing Games (or MMORPGs)—involve the creation and development of personalities or avatars. Many, although not all, MMORPGs are also violent in nature. Regardless of the nature of MMORPGs, they have one aspect in common: avatars evolve over time with continued play. The avatars cooperate and compete with one another in a constantly changing world. Once developed, players can sell their avatars on the Internet, for upward of thousands of dollars. Many of the "guilds," or online teams, in which these avatars exist require minimal levels of play. Some exceed 20 hours per week. The amount of skill and time needed to nurture high-valued avatars can become all-consuming. The Internet allows for 24-hour-a-day competition and communication with others of similar and higher skills and abilities all over the world.

The presence of computers, electronic devices, and the Internet in households today presents gaming opportunities at an unprecedented level. Children now begin using computers at very young ages. Even toddlers play on computers, smartphones, and tablets. In restaurants it's common to see young children occupied with electronic games while their parents eat in peace! Most children are familiar with electronic games by the time they reach elementary school, and teachers further encourage the use of electronics in completion of assignments. Many schools now integrate game-based apps into the teaching environment.

As children get older it becomes more and more difficult for their parents to regulate what they are doing online. In small doses, playing video games will clearly not cause harm, and you certainly have not damaged your children by letting them play in moderation. Occasional gaming is the norm, and some play may even be educational and healthy. Still, any behavior in excess can lead to difficulties. Excessive gaming can result in some potentially very dangerous consequences. The goals of this book are twofold: (1) to assist you in determining what level of playing is normal or acceptable for your child, and what degree of playing is—or is likely to become—problematic; and (2) to provide you with guidance on how to reduce gaming in your home once it has become too much.

Organization of the book

The first part of this book (Section 1) describes the research behind gaming. Internet gaming disorder is a condition gaining attention in medical communities worldwide. Parents interested in the science behind Internet gaming disorder will benefit from reading this section, which contains information related to background and research. Chapter 2 describes what Internet gaming disorder is and how common it is. Chapter 3 details how to distinguish a serious mental health condition related to gaming from regular or high levels of play that are not leading to difficulties. Chapter 4 outlines risk factors associated with development of Internet gaming disorder and addresses the link between gaming and violence. The last chapter in Section 1, Chapter 5, describes potential benefits your child may derive from gaming.

If you are primarily interested in what you can do to reduce problems with gaming and are less concerned about research and theory, you can skip directly to Section 2. This section offers ways to help your child decrease gaming. Chapter 6 provides advice about when you should intervene and the circumstances under which you should seek professional care for your child. Chapter 7 describes communication issues that impact not only your child's gaming behaviors, but also your relationship with your child more generally. Once you learn about communication styles, you will be able to discuss issues related to gaming with your child more effectively.

Chapters 8 to 10 outline three specific steps that you as a parent can take to minimize problems with your child's gaming: Record, Replace, and Reward. These three chapters provide specific and concrete examples of how to implement the steps and include worksheets to help you bring these principles into action. Chapter 11 addresses management of severe cases of Internet gaming disorder, and Chapter 12 prepares you to set reasonable expectations over the short and long term with respect to your child's gaming.

If you already know your child has problems with electronic games, or if you are worried that your child is on the road to developing them, you are not alone. Many parents of children and adolescents today share the same concerns. They are confused about why their children are so overtaken by these games and they want to know what they can do to minimize their children's gaming and the associated problems that can develop. By reading this book, you are already well on your way toward tackling these issues and helping your child. By implementing the steps this book describes, you can help your child, no matter what stage he or she is in. In the process, you may also find that you are helping yourself and improving your relationship with your child; to be sure, you are embarking on healthy change for your family and yourself.

BACKGROUND AND RESEARCH

2

What defines gaming problems, and how common are they?

You think your child is gaming more than his friends, and you know it is causing some problems with his schoolwork. You are constantly arguing with him about his gaming. You've even mentioned it to your pediatrician. The doctor didn't seem to take it very seriously, though, and said a lot of parents express concerns about video gaming but most kids grow out of it. Is this true, or is it possible that your child has a real problem with gaming?

Internet gaming disorder is a condition that relates to a group of behaviors that involve excessive and problematic play of electronic or video games. Most people with problems primarily play online, although problematic play can also occur offline and on devices other than computers. Excessive and problematic play can occur on any electronic device. For example, some people play on gaming consoles such as PlayStation, Wii, and Xbox, as well as on televisions. Others game on handheld devices, including Nintendo gaming consoles, tablets, and smartphones. The medium through which your child accesses electronic games does not impact the types of problems that develop. Nevertheless, online games—and specific types of online games—are most often associated with the development of difficulties.

The first part of this chapter describes terms applied to this condition. The second part outlines recent changes in technology that have impacted gaming and addresses the types of games that most often lead to problems. The chapter details the proportion of kids who have difficulties with gaming. Finally, it describes how often youth with problems recover from them and cease having difficulties with gaming.

Terminology

The word "disorder" means that symptoms have risen to a level that they are causing substantial difficulties. A number of labels describe excessive problems with gaming, such as "gaming addiction," "gaming disorder," "problem gaming," "compulsive gaming," "gaming dependence," "gaming abuse," "gaming use disorder," and "pathological gaming." Sometimes the word "Internet" occurs with the word "gaming." Examples are "Internet gaming addiction," "Internet gaming dependence," or "Internet gaming abuse."

At times, the word "gaming" is omitted from the phrase. "Internet addiction," "Internet dependence," and "pathologic Internet use" are common terms as well. In these cases, the activities may be more general and include chatting, using social media (such as Twitter and Instagram), or using the Internet for other purposes in conjunction with gaming. Excessive and problematic use of electronic media that does not include gaming may be distinct from gaming problems; the jury is still out on this issue. Regardless, the people most likely to develop significant problems with Internet use are those who play games on it.[1]

To minimize confusion over terminology, this book uses the phrase "Internet gaming disorder" when referring to a constellation of substantial problems that occur with game playing. This term is applied regardless of whether one accesses games online or otherwise. In other words, Internet gaming disorder refers to problems developing from any format of electronic or video game playing.

The types of problems that develop from Internet gaming disorder can be social, work- or school-related, physical and psychological, and even legal, in extreme cases. Many parents are also concerned that excessive playing of violent video games may lead to aggressive behavior in their kids. Although violent games are popular and certainly some kids with Internet gaming disorder exhibit aggression, most kids with the condition do not behave violently in real life. On the contrary, many adolescents and young adults with Internet gaming disorder are isolated and appear quite passive in their real-world interactions. Aggressive behaviors may occur in response to playing violent games, but violent actions are not necessary to classify a person with Internet gaming disorder. Chapter 4 describes the research on playing violent video games and violence.

The different names applied to this condition and the number and types of consequences to which it relates reflect a lack of agreement in the scientific community regarding what Internet gaming disorder is. This lack of consensus unfortunately limits our understanding about how widespread the condition is. Nevertheless, studies have begun to determine how many and how often young people, as well as adults, engage in problematic gaming.

Growth of the Internet and gaming

Access to computers and the Internet is increasing markedly throughout the world.[2] This growth has impacted electronic gaming. In 1997, only 37% of US households owned a computer, with just 18% having Internet access. By 2010, 77% of US households had one or more computers. The vast majority of homes now have Internet access. These rates are likely to continue increasing until they plateau at universal or near-universal coverage.

Other countries have paralleled or even exceeded these rates.[3] Less than 40% of Western European homes had Internet access in the early 2000s. Virtually none in Eastern European nations did. Today, over half of Eastern European households and more than 80% of European Union households connect to the Internet. Some

Asian countries have even higher levels of computer ownership and Internet access. The highest rates are in South Korea and Singapore. In these countries, over 88% of homes connect to the Internet. This rise in Internet usage worldwide has facilitated availability of electronic gaming. Although computers are often a medium through which kids play games, devices such as smartphones and tablets connect to the Internet and all its games as well. In addition, there are other devices designed exclusively for gaming. In the United States, a Nielsen report indicated that nearly 60% of households own a gaming console.[4] These include Wii, Xbox, or PlayStations. Handheld devices such as Nintendo are also popular, and gaming on cellular phones is rising dramatically.

Popularity of gaming and types of games

Given the popularity of electronic games, along with the penetration of the Internet into society and our homes, it is not surprising that our children play games electronically. Most children do. A survey of over 1000 randomly selected US youth between the ages of 8 and 18 found that 88% of them played games electronically.[5] The majority reported frequent gaming. Over two-thirds (68%) of kids indicate that they play video games at least once or twice a week, and 23% play them daily. The average amount of time kids game is about 12 hours a week.[6] A detailed monitoring study found that on average kids played about 1 hour per day on weekdays, and even longer on weekends.[7] The proportions of kids who game, and game frequently, are similarly high or even higher in other countries.[8]

Kids game frequently, and there is a wide variety of games to choose from. Old-fashioned ones you may remember like Pong, Pac-Man, and Donkey Kong still exist, but they are no longer very popular. Youth today are more likely to play fighting games. These include realistic first-person shooter games that are extremely "upfront and personal," like Halo and Call of Duty. Third-person shooter games are more tactical in nature, and in these games (e.g., Dead Space, Resident Evil, and Gears of War) players see characters from a distance. In addition to fighting games, there are also simulation, sports, strategy, and construction games. Some of the most popular online games today are World of Warcraft, League of Legends, Halo 4, The Sims 3, FIFA 13, StarCraft 2, and Minecraft. In World of Warcraft, players battle human and computer opponents. Over 12 million people regularly play this game, and it accounts for over half of the online video game market at the time of this writing. Another battle game, League of Legends, by some accounts is now surpassing World of Warcraft in popularity. Players of Halo 4, yet another popular fighting game, become soldiers, and they attempt to destroy alien races by competing or cooperating with one another. In contrast, The Sims 3 involves a virtual world or civilization. Characters work and socialize with one another online. In FIFA, individuals join soccer teams, and they compete against other teams. StarCraft 2 is a strategy game; it involves players multitasking to obtain resources, assemble an army, and penetrate the defense of opposing armies. Minecraft is a very popular construction game in which players acquire resources to build and sustain a virtual world. Of all game genres, the multiplayer ones are most likely to lead to problems.

World of Warcraft is a specific type of multiplayer game known as an MMORPG. The first of such games was launched in Korea in 1995, and the number of these games and people playing them has increased markedly since then. Estimates indicate over 19 million people subscribe to at least one MMORPG. As noted earlier, MMORPGs consist of sophisticated, detailed, and evolving "worlds." In these virtual communities, players assume roles that relate to virtual personae, or avatars, such as warriors or magicians. The players collaborate with others in guilds to accomplish missions. They have "powers" to talk online, make friends, and conduct transactions involving real or virtual assets. Players in World of Warcraft, for example, may spend days or even weeks hunting for a special item;

the chances of uncovering it may be as low as 0.01%. The rarity of the items or events, along with the difficulties of acquiring them, provides players who obtain these items with a very special, and highly desired, status. Many adolescents and even adults seek this type of excitement and status. The more they play, the better they can become. High-scoring players achieve stardom, and many child and adult players alike follow these stars' performance. Your child can view experts playing specific games online[9] to learn the tricks of the trade. Gamers idolize top players of online games just as some people idolize famous athletes. There are tournaments and championships, with professional commentators and advertising sponsors.[10] Some championships boast hundreds of thousands of viewers.[11] The winners can be awarded very large sums of money, which, not surprisingly, has made wagering on players' performance commonplace. However, unlike the Super Bowl or World Series, gaming competitions are not limited by country. Top players travel around the world to matches, and they are afforded celebrity status. Instead of dreaming about becoming the next football or baseball star, some kids nowadays are fantasizing about becoming gaming stars.

Prevalence rates of Internet gaming disorder

Many kids and adults enjoy playing MMORPGs and other types of games electronically, and most do not become consumed by them or develop problems with them. So, how common are these problems?

Prevalence rate is a term that describes the proportion of a given population that has a condition such as Internet gaming disorder. To establish accurate prevalence rates of Internet gaming disorder, surveys conducted with large numbers of people are needed. The people in the surveys should be representative of the general population, which means that they should not vary in any systematic way from people not participating in the survey.

Studies of prevalence rates of Internet gaming disorder do exist.[12] However, the definitions and classifications of gaming problems vary across these studies, resulting in a substantial variation in estimated prevalence rates. Some studies report rates of gaming problems in less than 2% of the population.[13] Others note rates of more than 8%,[14] depending on how the condition is defined. As described within the DSM-5 and assessed in studies to date, Internet gaming disorder probably affects about 1.5% of youth.

Most likely, rates differ so dramatically and are much higher in some studies because of the ways researchers assess gaming problems. Many youth readily acknowledge gaming until late in the night or longer than they planned. Lots of kids argue with their parents about their game playing from time to time. These behaviors do not necessarily reflect serious problems. For example, "Do you sometimes skip household chores in order to spend more time playing video games?" was an item used to assess problems in one study, which found relatively high prevalence rates.[15] Avoiding chores is likely not indicative of real problems with gaming (after all, who doesn't avoid chores once in a while?). Prevalence rates are artificially high when items reflecting mild symptoms are used. If you are interested in exactly how to assess Internet gaming disorder in your child, Chapter 3 describes the symptoms. Chapter 6 includes a self-test for kids, along with a parental version to check for gaming problems in younger children.

Even if the true rates of Internet gaming disorder are on the lower end of the range in research studies—around 1.5%—these rates are important. For example, the prevalence rates of schizophrenia and cocaine use disorder are under 1%. Still, these disorders are major public health concerns. Even though they affect less than 1 in 100 people, these disorders represent significant burdens for the people suffering from them, their family members, and society at large. As research develops on Internet gaming disorder, a better understanding of this condition, its prevalence rate, and its consequences will emerge. In the meantime, any child has about a 1.5% chance of having a problem with gaming. Rates are even higher among kids with certain characteristics, such as having some psychological conditions. Chapter 4 describes factors that increase your child's likelihood of having Internet gaming disorder.

The natural course of Internet gaming disorder

If you suspect that your child already has Internet gaming disorder, it can be useful to understand how gaming problems change over time. For example, if gaming problems dissipate over time in most kids even without treatment, then you may not want or need to seek professional care for your child. If your child is likely to mature out of gaming problems on his own, then there is no need to do anything deliberate right now. On the other hand, if gaming problems most often persist or worsen over time, then you probably will want to seek professional treatment for your child as soon as possible.

Unfortunately, little is known about how gaming problems change over time. The few studies that have investigated this issue found that between 35% and 86% of kids continued having problems with gaming over a 1.5- to 2-year period.[16] Therefore, if your child has Internet gaming disorder right now, he or she likely has at least a one-in-three chance of continuing to have problems over the next couple years if you do not get some sort of treatment or intervention.

By better understanding how Internet gaming disorder is assessed, you will be in a better position to decide whether your child might be in this "problem group" and could benefit from treatment. Even if your child has only minor problems with gaming right now, it is still important to know how to recognize more severe difficulties if they progress. The next chapter describes issues related to assessment and diagnosis of Internet gaming disorder.

3

How can I check for Internet gaming disorder in my child?

Your neighbor's son has an extreme problem with gaming. He nearly failed out of high school, never went to college, and then lost his job, all because of gaming. He now just stays home playing video games all day. Your son, fortunately, is not failing out of school; in fact, he has always done fairly well academically. However, all his free time is monopolized by gaming. He doesn't want to get a summer job because it may take away from his gaming time, and he plans to make money playing online video games instead. His gaming is causing arguments at home, and he seems to have few real friends. All he talks about are the games. How can you know whether your child has Internet gaming disorder? Can he even have such a condition if his problems aren't as severe as those of your neighbor's son?

As a parent, you may already know that your child has severe problems related to gaming. You don't have to be a doctor to know something is seriously wrong when your child has dropped out of school to play video games all day. On the other hand, you may be uncertain about the severity or extent of your child's difficulties with gaming. Remember that regular gaming is the norm, not the exception, in today's society. Many parents want to know where their child falls in relation to others in terms of the severity of the problem, and whether or when they should intervene and seek professional advice.

Even if your child does have severe gaming problems and you bring him to a psychiatrist or psychologist, he may not receive a diagnosis of Internet gaming disorder. Because Internet gaming disorder is not included in the official manual of psychiatric conditions used by mental health professionals nationally, the *Diagnostic and Statistical Manual of Mental Disorders* (DSM), the medical profession does not officially recognize this condition.

The most recent revision of the DSM, published in 2013 (known as DSM-5), lists Internet gaming disorder in a section of the manual called the research appendix. Although not listed as a formal diagnosis, the fact of its inclusion in the manual represents a major advance for recognition of the condition. The appendix of the DSM-5 includes conditions that *may be* psychiatric or mental diseases, but for which scientific data are not yet well established. Given the nascent nature of this area, more research is needed to reliably diagnose the condition. Research must determine how to differentiate kids who suffer significant consequences from those who do not. For example, most youth who game—even those who game a lot—do not have a significant problem that warrants a formal diagnosis. A child may game 3 or more hours a day but still not experience any serious difficulties because of gaming.

Research has also not yet established whether Internet gaming disorder is a unique mental disorder or a reflection of other overlapping conditions. In other words, we don't know if all or almost all kids who have gaming problems also have another condition, such as attention deficit hyperactivity disorder (ADHD), social phobia, or depression. If so, then excessive gaming may be a symptom of the other disorder, and not itself a stand-alone diagnosis. Regardless of whether it is a mental disorder or not, the signs and symptoms of Internet gaming disorder reflect problems that can arise as a result of excessive gaming.

DSM-5 criteria for Internet gaming disorder

It can be useful for you as a parent to understand the DSM-5 criteria for Internet gaming disorder so that you can better understand your child's behaviors in relation to these symptoms. The nine criteria in the DSM-5[1] are:

- Preoccupation with gaming
- Withdrawal symptoms
- Tolerance for gaming or excitement derived from games
- Unsuccessful attempts to reduce or stop gaming
- Gives up other activities to game
- Continues despite problems with gaming
- Deceives or covers up gaming
- Escapes adverse moods by gaming
- Risks or loses relationships or opportunities

Parents do not "diagnose" their children, but they know more about their children's behavior than anyone else. As you read through this section, you might consider the extent to which these symptoms apply to your child. Understanding the system by which professionals classify mental disorders may help put you at ease if these examples do not apply to your child. However, if your child appears to be a "textbook" case of Internet gaming disorder, you may want to seek professional services.

Remember, too, that even professionals do not yet agree on how to diagnose Internet gaming disorder. Researchers and clinicians are studying these criteria and symptoms. They may change over time.

With these caveats in mind, the following sections describe the nine DSM-5 criteria or symptoms for Internet gaming disorder as they currently exist.[2] Although there are nine, please note that having just a couple of them does not mean your child has the condition. The DSM-5 suggests that five out of nine symptoms are needed for a diagnosis, an issue further elaborated on in the last section of this chapter. The goal now is to better understand the criteria for Internet gaming disorder so that you can better evaluate your child's behavior. You can begin to consider whether your child's game playing is similar to or different from that of people with problems severe enough to warrant a diagnosis.

Preoccupation

A primary criterion of Internet gaming disorder relates to being preoccupied with gaming. Preoccupation refers to spending excessive amounts of time thinking about games. It also relates to planning when one can play again. For example, while in school, a child may keep thinking about mistakes she made in a past game. Instead of paying attention to her teacher, she may consider new strategies to correct them as soon as she can get home and back into the game.

To meet the criterion, preoccupation should go beyond times in which your child is actively gaming. Kids are often totally immersed in a game while playing it. The nature of these games is to draw total attention. To meet this criterion, your child must be thinking about playing, fantasizing about playing, or perseverating about games, even when involved in other activities. Some people report that their entire lives begin to focus around gaming. As soon as they awaken in the morning, they want to start playing. At school, their minds consistently drift back to their preferred game and what they are going to do or try next. Dylan is an example.

> Dylan is a 15-year-old boy who spends about 5 hours a day online playing World of Warcraft. When he is at school, he keeps thinking back to the game he played the night before, and how he could have done things differently. He thinks about how he is going to react in the afternoon, as soon as he can get back online. He is distracted in class, considering his next moves and new scenarios that may evolve as soon as he can get back into the game. At lunchtime and between classes, he is bored with most conversations. He is only interested in talking with the one or two other kids at his school who are serious World of Warcraft players. Their discussions solely involve the game.

Surveys on Internet gaming disorder find that people commonly report preoccupation with gaming, meaning that it is a mild to moderate symptom. In fact, 5% to 21% of kids state they feel preoccupied with gaming.[3] Although many youth admit to preoccupation with games, only 1% to 2% have Internet gaming disorder, as Chapter 2 describes. This symptom (or any symptom) alone is not indicative of having Internet gaming disorder. Your child needs to have at least five symptoms for the condition. This chapter later describes this issue in more depth.

Withdrawal

Withdrawal symptoms in gaming disorder may include irritability, anger, anxiety, restlessness, sadness, and depression. If an inability to game for several days in a row leads to these symptoms in your child, then he may be experiencing withdrawal from gaming.

It is important to distinguish withdrawal symptoms from the natural reactions that result from being prevented or stopped from doing any enjoyable or fun activity. Most children experience strong emotional reactions when a parent interrupts their games. These reactions can be intense! You can certainly relate to the extreme irritability, anger, and frustration that result when you ask your child to stop playing in order to eat dinner or go to bed. Similarly, leaving the television in the middle of a show is difficult. An outburst in relation to shutting off a television program, however, does not reflect withdrawal from television viewing.

Withdrawal from gaming can relate to symptoms that occur when your child is trying to stop or reduce gaming. Withdrawal can also manifest when a naturally occurring situation prevents your child from gaming for substantial periods of time. Being unable to play for several days due to a computer breakdown is an example. Of course, anger and irritability can also arise if you as a parent take your child's game, computer, or iPhone away. The key difference is that withdrawal refers to symptoms that are present when gaming is not possible or when your child attempts to stop playing on his own.

Reactions or outbursts in response to a parent insisting that play stop do not constitute withdrawal symptoms. Consider this next case.

Kevin is a 13-year-old who spends much of his time playing online sports games. He rushes home from school to play each day, and plays until late in the evening. He has achieved extraordinarily high scores, and he is very proud of them. He dreams of becoming the next worldwide star of FIFA 13. Kevin's parents bring him to his grandparents' house one weekend, and they do not have Internet access. Even though he brings his own computer to their home, Kevin is unable to play his favorite game without the Internet. Kevin spends the weekend sulking and angry. He cannot believe his parents made him come here, with no ability to play. Even though his grandfather bought him tickets to see a professional football game on Saturday, Kevin does not want to go. He wants his grandfather to bring him to a Wi-Fi-enabled coffee shop instead, so he can access the Internet and catch up with his games. His grandfather is completely dumbfounded that Kevin does not want to go see the Steelers play, even though they have always been his favorite team. When he asks Kevin why he doesn't want to go, Kevin gets angry and screams, "Can't you just bring me somewhere I can get online? If you want to do something with me that I like, that is what I want to do. That will make me happy! Why can't you understand?"

Kevin may be experiencing withdrawal symptoms after being unable to access games. His grandparents were not explicitly preventing him from playing; Kevin was just unable to get online during the weekend. His inability to play thwarted him from doing something he normally would have loved doing—going to a professional football game.

In this case, Kevin was not trying to reduce his game playing. Withdrawal symptoms can also occur when people try to reduce or cut back on gaming on their own. Consider the case of Michelle.

Michelle is a 20-year-old college sophomore who spends much of her time playing Call of Duty online. Although it typically appeals more to males, she loves the attention she gets playing, and competing with and doing better than most boys. Michelle plays every night, and she considers playing to be her reward for completing an assignment or a way of celebrating after taking an exam. When Michelle received her course grades at the end of the fall semester, she was very disappointed. She realized she was spending too much time playing and not enough on her course work. She was now at risk of having to spend another whole year at school if her grades did not improve. She made a vow to herself to reduce how much she played in the spring semester until her grades got better. She was only going to play on the weekends, and only if she had finished all her home-work and didn't have an important exam in the upcoming week.

Rather than studying more, Michelle found she was getting very anxious. She could not concentrate while she was trying to study. She was angry that she had no outlet to relax since she was holding firm to her commitment to reduce gaming. The weekdays would go by, and even though she was no longer gaming, she wasn't getting her assignments done, or at least not done well. She didn't let herself play much even on the weekends, because she had so much work to do left over from the week. She spent the weekends feeling stressed, sad, lonely, and even worthless. She started to wonder if she were better off returning to gaming, as her grades did not seem to be improving.

Michelle, unlike Kevin, recognized that gaming was causing problems in her life. As Michelle was attempting to reduce her gaming, she felt anxious, irritable, and depressed—hallmark with-drawal symptoms.

Withdrawal is one of the least common symptoms of gaming disorder, and less than 5% report it in most surveys.[4] Most people who experience withdrawal have many other symptoms as well.[5] Therefore, if your child does have withdrawal symptoms, this can be a reason for concern.

Tolerance

Tolerance refers to needing increasingly more of something to achieve the desired effect. An example that most people can easily understand relates to alcohol. A person with an alcohol use disorder may drink five or more alcoholic beverages to feel the effects—and that number increases over time. In contrast, a social drinker may find that one or two drinks are sufficient to stimulate pleasant feelings.

In the context of gaming, tolerance refers to the need to play games for longer periods to become excited by them or to feel as though goals have been accomplished within them. Consider a young person who used to limit playing to weekends or occasional weeknights. If this person is now playing every day and for long periods each day in order to feel a sense of excitement or satisfaction with gaming, this pattern reflects tolerance.

Because gaming is an engrossing activity, it is easy to misconstrue tolerance. Kids can, and do, spend hours each day gaming. The amount of time your child spends playing has probably increased over time, as it would for any hobby in which he shows an interest. Gaming is a popular pastime, and one reason kids play so much is because they like it. That is not tolerance.

Tolerance is not defined by a specific amount of time. Some people game for 6 or more hours at a time, but they do so because they *want* to be playing that long. They are not playing that long because it takes hours of play to feel excited or experience satisfaction from playing.

Relatively few people report this symptom when it includes explicit references to needing to game for longer periods to feel excited.[6] When defined in this manner, this symptom is important in distinguishing kids with and without Internet gaming disorder.[7]

Unsuccessful attempts to stop or cut back

Another symptom of Internet gaming disorder is a desire, but inability, to stop or reduce gaming. This implies that one is motivated or has made attempts to stop or cut back. Trying, or desiring, to change presumes that someone has experienced adverse consequences. At least on some level, the person recognizes that the behavior is excessive.

Successful attempts to reduce, or actually stop, gaming do not reflect the symptom. Consider a teenager who recognized that his playing League of Legends was impeding his ability to do his homework, so he stopped playing. If he were able to limit gaming to certain days or times, he also would not meet the criterion. In both these cases, he does not have *unsuccessful* attempts to cease or reduce playing. On the contrary, his attempts are successful.

Returning to the case of Michelle, she recognized that her game playing was causing problems with her college course work. After several weeks of trying not to play games, Michelle returned to frequent gaming even though she truly did not want to be playing so often. She continuously regretted her decisions to play. She is an example of someone with this symptom.

Most people with addictions *do* desire to quit or reduce their problem behavior from time to time. Up to one in five drinkers report this in regard to their alcohol use.[8] Similarly, youth often admit to making attempts to cease or reduce their gaming.[9] Being repeatedly unsuccessful in these attempts reflects an important aspect of Internet gaming disorder.

Loss of interest in other hobbies

This symptom relates to engaging in one behavior to the exclusion of other social or recreational activities. An example is a child who used to play baseball or soccer. Now, he only games electronically. He gave up playing sports completely because of his gaming.

However, not all kids are involved in structured or healthy extracurricular activities to give up. In fact, this symptom can be turned around: a risk factor for developing Internet gaming disorder is a lack of other recreational pursuits.[10] Without other activities to give up, it would be difficult to conclude that your child is giving up other activities to play games. Consider the case of a teenage boy, Jeremy.

Jeremy goes to school, but he is not involved in any sports, music, or organized activities. When school is over, he comes home, typically to an empty house because both his parents work. When Jeremy arrives home at 3 p.m. he watches television or turns on the computer and begins gaming until his mom or dad gets home at about 6 p.m. One of his parents usually makes dinner, and then they eat, often in front of the TV. After dinner Jeremy goes to his room to play games until he falls asleep, often very late at night.

On the one hand, you may think that Jeremy's behavior reflects giving up other activities in favor of video games. He does little other than play video games. On the other hand, Jeremy may be playing games simply to fill unoccupied time. If this is the case and his gaming is not preventing him from doing other things, then he is not really giving anything up to play games. He would not qualify as having this symptom.

Now think about another situation:

Kara used to spend most of her free time with girlfriends. They would go to one another's houses after school. They would text frequently and communicate by social media in the evenings. On weekends, Kara used to go to parties or movies with friends. Now, she primarily just plays video games alone at home and has little contact with her old friends.

Because Kara began neglecting her real-life friends due to all the time she was spending gaming, she does have this symptom of gaming addiction. A hallmark of addiction is a focus on the problematic activity while giving up other hobbies and pastimes.

Only about 1.5% of youth have this symptom in relation to gaming.[11] If your child used to be involved in a larger number of activities but now is engaging in very few recreational or social activities, or none at all other than gaming, then she or he has this symptom.

Persistent gaming despite problems

This symptom relates to continuing to play games, even when the gamer recognizes that problems have arisen from his or her play. Difficulties related to gaming can include issues at school or work, with friends or family, or with psychological or physical health. Although far less common, some people also have legal or financial issues related to gaming. These types of problems can occur in a number of contexts, including:

- **School.** The most typical problems in school-aged children relate to not doing homework or doing poorly on tests due to excessive gaming. They can also include oversleeping and being late for school because of late-night gaming episodes.
- **Family.** Problems can also arise with family members due to gaming. For children and younger adolescents, concerns are most likely to arise with parents. Parents may attempt to control or limit the amount of time their child spends gaming. These attempts to restrain playing time can lead to arguments, which can become regular and even intense.
- **Social.** Excessive gaming can also lead to disagreements with friends or others. For example, friends (or coworkers for adults) may start criticizing one's gaming. The outcomes of games or amount of time spent gaming may lead to serious disputes. The previous criterion (loss of interest in other hobbies) relates to spending less time with friends or others on nongaming social and recreational activities. Thus, socializing less with others should not be considered as an aspect of both criteria. This criterion, rather, refers to problems

getting along with others, to social problems specifically—not just to spending less time in social situations.

- **Physical.** Repeated fast movements on keyboards and joysticks can lead to soreness and stiffness in hands, fingers, or wrists. Backaches can occur from tense muscles. In one study of online gamers,[12] over 35% reported sore eyes, carpal tunnel syndrome, back pain, or other physical problems. Thirty percent indicated they had been sleeping less because of gaming. Although such physical symptoms are common, they need to lead to *significant* physical or health impairment to reflect this symptom. A temporary and nonproblematic lack of sleep, stiff wrists, or back strains do not mean that someone has a gaming problem.
- **Financial.** Some people spend excessive amounts of money on games. They may buy lots of software or hardware for games, pay for multiple gaming subscriptions, or purchase avatars or chances to win rare items online. If the amount of money spent on gaming is causing financial or even legal difficulties (e.g., your child stole a credit card to pay for his gaming), your child has this symptom.

If you are having regular arguments with your child about gaming and they are adversely impacting your relationship or the family more generally, that is problematic and represents the symptom of persistent gaming despite problems. Similarly, if your child repeatedly receives poor grades or is regularly late to school or with homework assignments due to gaming, he or she has this symptom.

On the other hand, occasional arguments, loss of sleep, incomplete assignments, or stiff wrists that do not lead to adverse consequences are not a sign of gaming difficulties. In a US study, over 20% of youth reported skipping homework assignments and doing poorly on a school assignment or test because they spent too much time gaming.[13] Occasional family disagreements over gaming are also commonplace.[14] However, getting into *trouble* at school or work because of gaming or having *serious* fights or arguments about gaming are less common. Less than 2% of youth report these more severe symptoms.[15] They clearly indicate problems.

Deceit

Deceiving others about the extent of a problem behavior is something that occurs in all addictions. It is not uncommon for adolescents to keep hidden the amount of time they are spending online from their parents. A single instance of lying or covering up gaming is not sufficient to constitute this symptom, but repeatedly lying or covering up gaming activities is indicative of a problem. Studies find that about 3% to 14% of youth report covering up or lying about their gaming.[16]

Escape

Kids may game to avoid thinking about or dealing with important issues in their lives. They may play to get through a difficult day or situation. Gaming may also mask feelings of helplessness, guilt, worry, anxiety, stress, or depression. Consider this example.

Olivia is a college student who spends upwards of 8 hours a day playing Candy Crush on her iPhone. She plays between classes and for hours into the night. She started playing her first year in college. She lives with her parents, and the campus is about an hour from her home. There was a lot of free time between her classes, during which she had little to do. She discovered the game, and something about it really appealed to her. However, she is now finding that she wants to play even when she is not between classes. Whenever she gets into an argument with her parents, she finds herself playing. She often stays late at the college playing in the library or in her car so she can avoid going home and talking with her parents. When she has a bad day or gets a poor grade, she comforts herself and forgets about her problems by playing. Achieving a high score makes her feel better. Playing helps her to stop thinking how poorly she is doing in school.

If your child games to forget about problems, he or she is not alone. Up to 31% of youth game to escape negative moods or to avoid unpleasant situations.[17] In other words, many kids report this symptom, but this symptom alone does not signal substantial problems with gaming. If your child does not have multiple other problems, playing games to mask bad feelings is fairly normal. However, when it occurs with multiple other symptoms, then it can signal more severe problems with gaming.

Jeopardized or lost a relationship, job, or educational or career opportunity

The most extreme consequence of addictive disorders is losing someone or something important.[18] In the case of Internet gaming disorder, it is clear that some kids do drop out of school because their game playing becomes so excessive. There are also cases of excessive gaming leading to suicide attempts, violence, and even death, even though the vast majority of cases do not rise to this level.

On the other hand, a child can lie to his parents about the amount of time he is playing games (deceit) without breaking relationships with his parents entirely. Repeated arguments about gaming are common. They do not necessarily destroy or jeopardize the relationship between parent and child. Likewise, a child may game excessively knowing that it is causing some difficulties at school although she may not lose out on an important educational prospect. Risking an educational opportunity goes beyond failing to complete a homework assignment or doing poorly on a test. It refers to failing a course, achieving much lower than usual semester grades, being suspended from school for being late or missing too many days, or dropping out of school completely because of gaming.

As you might expect, risking or losing something or someone important is the least common symptom related to Internet gaming disorder.[19] Typically, only about 1% of people report risking or losing relationships or work or school opportunities due to gaming. If your child has experienced this severe a consequence, it is likely that she or he has other symptoms of Internet gaming disorder as well.

Early warning signs, or symptoms

It is important for you as a parent to know about the problems that can occur with gaming, what they might look like in real life, and how significant they can become. Although you will never "diagnose" your child, you can use the descriptions of symptoms in this book as a guide. Chapter 6 provides questionnaires that screen for these symptoms, which you may use when deciding whether to seek professional help.

The DSM-5 suggests that people should meet at least five out of the nine criteria before a mental health professional can diagnose them with Internet gaming disorder. This is a conservative threshold, designed to ensure that only kids who really have problems receive a diagnosis. But even if your child does not have five or more symptoms, you may have spotted some familiar behaviors in the previous sections of this chapter, and your child can still benefit from the strategies outlined later. The prognosis or course of most conditions is better the sooner help is provided. This is likely the case for Internet gaming disorder as well. However, to intervene early requires that the condition be identified in its less severe forms. It is imperative, therefore, that you as a parent recognize early the signs and symptoms of this condition in your child. By knowing how to look for problems, even relatively mild and early-stage symptoms, you will be in a better position to reverse or prevent more significant adverse effects. If your child is suffering from severe and full-blown gaming problems and has five or more of the symptoms, it is not too late to take action to reverse the extent of these problems.

4

Are some kids more likely to develop Internet gaming disorder? Understanding risk factors

Stephanie's daughter, Molly, has always been a bit unusual. From an early age, she was more interested in "boys' games" than in dolls or girls' activities. She has been socially awkward and a loner since elementary school. She was diagnosed with mild autism and attention deficit disorder when she was 8, and she's never done well in school. Although Stephanie got Molly all the special help she could, Molly barely keeps up and has a lot of difficulties passing courses. She loves that she excels at Grand Theft Auto, and it seems to be the one thing she is proud of herself for. She doesn't seem to have any real friends from school, but she does talk about gaming friends. Stephanie doesn't want to take away any successes her daughter feels, but she fears she may develop a problem if she continues to game as much as she has been. Molly is now playing at least a couple of hours every day and often late at night. There are a lot of mental health problems in Stephanie's family, and Molly's father's side is full of alcoholism. Is Molly at heightened risk for Internet gaming disorder?

Does my child have any predispositions for Internet gaming disorder?

Certain characteristics or environmental situations put some people at higher risk than others for developing gaming problems—these are called "risk factors." The frequency and duration of time spent gaming is one potential risk factor. Specific types of games are linked

35

with a greater likelihood of problems as well. Boys are more likely to have difficulties with gaming than girls, but certainly girls can develop gaming problems as well. Some studies have found that kids from minority backgrounds may also be at higher risk for gaming problems; the reasons for this are most likely very complex, but scientists do have some theories that are outlined below. In addition, kids with depression and those with less developed social skills may experience problems with gaming at high rates, as may those with impulsivity and ADHD. Adolescents and young adults who drink alcohol or use illegal drugs also appear to have higher rates of gaming problems than those who do not.

The first part of this chapter identifies and explains risk factors associated with Internet gaming disorder. The second part addresses a related concern many parents have: the possible connection between aggressive tendencies or violence and gaming.

Risk factors for gaming problems

Play-related risk factors

Clearly, kids who play games daily or almost daily are more likely to have problems with gaming than those who rarely play. Youth who game for long durations are also more likely to experience problems than are those who game for short periods. Nevertheless, frequency and duration of play are not diagnostic criteria for Internet gaming disorder. They are correlated with—but not always indicative of— problems.[1] For example, addicted gamers play more than twice as long on average (25 hours each week) than their nonaddicted peers (12 hours).[2] Nevertheless, some kids who are not addicted play for even longer periods each week. And, even if your child plays for less than 25 hours a week, he may still have significant problems arising from gaming.

Certain games in particular seem to foster problems. MMORPG players game more frequently than players of games that do not require regular or consistent play to make progress.[3] World of Warcraft players spend more time gaming than players of any other game, with an average of 3 hours per day.[4] One survey[5] even reported an average of 63 hours per week of play among MMORPG players! Players of MMORPGs also have higher rates of gaming problems than players of other games.[6] Another study[7] asked young adults to play MMORPGs or other types of games for a month. Those who played MMORPGs ended up playing more hours and developing poorer health and sleep, and had greater difficulties with "real-life" socializing and academic work, than did players of any other type of game. Thus, MMORPGs represent a potentially dangerous format. If your child plays MMORPGs and has experienced some adverse effects from gaming, you certainly have cause for concern. However, even if your child does not play MMORPGs, he still may have problems with gaming. Gamers of all genres can and do develop Internet gaming disorder.

Demographic risk factors

Male gender. Boys are 5.5 times more likely than girls to play MMORPGs, and two-thirds of boys game at least weekly versus less than half of girls.[8] Boys also have a 2- to 10-fold increased risk of gaming problems compared with girls.[9]

Gender differences in gaming problems are not surprising, but girls and women can also develop difficulties with gaming. Gaming to regulate moods, lack of other social activities, problems in school, and low social skills are closely related to gaming problems. These issues may be as or more important than gender when considering risk factors.[10]

Age. Age is another important factor. Younger people, and especially adolescent boys, game more often than any other group.[11] Young males are also the group most likely to develop problems with gaming.[12] Older adolescents game slightly less often than younger children, but durations of playing are longer in older adolescents, and rates of problems are generally similar in younger and older adolescents.[13] Although frequencies and durations of play may differ at various developmental stages, kids of any age, as well as adults, can have problems with gaming.

Culture and race/ethnicity. In the United States, racial and ethnic minority youth, including Asian Americans, have been shown to have higher rates of gaming problems than Caucasian youth.[14] Similarly, youth residing in European countries who were born outside Europe have higher rates of gaming problems than do native-born European youth.[15] This association may relate in part to socioeconomic status, as immigrants are often overrepresented in lower-socioeconomic-status groups.

Media reports indicate extraordinarily high rates of problems with Internet use generally—and Internet gaming specifically—in some Southeast Asian countries. In response to this epidemic, the Chinese government banned console games between 2000 and 2015. China also instituted a system to monitor the playing time of children. When youth spent more than 3 hours online in 1 day, the system turned off in-game reward mechanisms or stopped play entirely. Similarly, in South Korea, the Ministry of Culture, Sports and Tourism had popular game sites prevent players under 18 years of age from gaming after midnight.

Although Southeast Asian countries report high rates of gaming problems and "Internet addiction" generally, cultural differences may impact the perception of problems. For example, in some Southeast Asian countries, parents may consider any screen time that interferes with schoolwork or family time to be very troubling, while using electronics for recreation is the norm in US families.

Psychological risk factors

Regardless of demographic characteristics such as gender, age, and race/ethnicity, your child is at greater risk for gaming difficulties if she or he has mental health issues. Emotional conditions such as depression and anxiety, and impulse control disorders such as attention deficit disorder, are linked with gaming problems. Kids who have difficulties socially also tend to be more likely to have gaming problems.

Depression and social competence. Problem gamers have higher rates of depression than do their gaming peers,[16] and this relationship goes in both directions. In other words, spending more time gaming can lead to greater depression, and increases in depression over time can also lead to heavier gaming.[17] This relationship is important, because if your child has Internet gaming disorder, it is likely he also has some symptoms of depression. Even if your child does not have Internet gaming disorder and is not depressed right now, depression later in adolescence or during early adulthood may signal an increase in gaming problems at that time. At the same time, an increase in gaming problems down the road is likely to result in greater depression symptoms too.

Because of the consistent association between depression and gaming problems, antidepressants have been tested for, and may reduce, both types of symptoms.[18] However, well-controlled studies have yet to examine how well antidepressants work for gaming disorder specifically. If your child has symptoms of both depression and Internet gaming disorder, medication for depression may have the added benefit of also decreasing gaming problems.

Difficulties with social situations are also associated with gaming problems. As gaming increases, social anxiety can rise and the quality of interpersonal relationships can decrease.[19] At the same time, kids who are socially isolated or who have poor interpersonal skills may be especially drawn to aspects of video games. Many games foster online relationships and allow players to take on new personalities. People with social phobia are uncomfortable in interpersonal situations involving face-to-face contact, but they may derive positive experiences from remote and anonymous communications that occur in online games.

Kids have many other reasons for playing electronic games, and their motivations for playing may affect their chances of developing problems with gaming. Although social reasons are primary for some kids, others game mainly to feel a sense of achievement. They gain power or status online. They may also enjoy making complex decisions or competing against others. Finally, others may play primarily to escape. They like taking on fantasy roles or may play to avoid real-life problems or concerns. Boys are more likely to play MMORPGs to achieve feelings of power or status, while girls play more for social reasons. Playing to escape is linked with the development of gaming problems regardless of gender.[20]

In sum, depression and social competence are related to Internet gaming disorder, and these relationships seem to go in both directions. Depression and social difficulties may draw one in to gaming. Conversely, gaming excessively may lead to greater feelings of depression and social isolation. If your child is depressed or socially anxious or isolated and has problems with gaming, helping her to reduce gaming may assist in alleviating some of her depression and social anxiety symptoms as well. Similarly, effective treatment for depression or social anxiety, through the help of a mental health professional, may reduce your child's gaming behaviors and symptoms as well.

Impulsivity and ADHD. Impulsivity and ADHD are also related to Internet gaming disorder. Youth with gaming problems have more impulse-control difficulties than youth without gaming problems.[21] Kids with ADHD in particular may be highly susceptible to developing gaming problems.[22] On the other hand, children who spend increasing amounts of time gaming also develop more attention problems, indicating that difficulties with attention may also *arise from* heavy gaming.[23]

Preliminary studies show that medication for ADHD may reduce gaming symptoms.[24] If your child has ADHD or other attention problems, it is important to have him assessed and treated for this condition, using medication (if appropriate) or psychotherapy, or both. Chapter 6 discusses issues related to professional treatment in more depth.

Substance use. Gaming is also linked to substance use. Youth with gaming problems are more likely to report drinking, smoking, and/or marijuana use than those without gaming problems.[25] Therefore, if your child has a gaming problem, he may also be at greater risk for smoking or using substances. The link between substance use and gaming may be in part biological. Brain regions that respond to urges or desires to use drugs also appear to respond to gaming images and urges.[26]

Parents of adolescents and young adults should consider whether their child is experimenting with substances. Some parents feel that gaming is less of a concern than substance use, and in some cases, it certainly is. However, the earlier kids start using drugs and alcohol, the greater their likelihood of developing problems with them.[27] As a parent of a child with gaming problems, you certainly want to be aware of the possibility of substance use problems—both now and in the future. You will want to address or seek help for any substance-use issues as soon as you detect them. See Chapter 6 for advice related to seeking professional help.

Aggression and gaming

The possible link between video game playing and aggression has generated a lot of controversy. The consensus among scientists and mental health professionals is that playing violent video games *may* be associated with increased violent behavior in some, but certainly not in all, players. A connection between playing violent video games and aggression is not definitively established, but its possibility warrants concern.

Research[28] conducted on this issue suggests that exposure to violent video games appears to be related to aggressive behaviors, thoughts, and affect (mood), but not necessarily to delinquency or criminal behaviors. Playing violent video games may also lead to reduced empathy and social behaviors. These associations appear consistent across cultures and genders. One study[29] even showed that high rates of violent video game playing resulted in increased aggressive behaviors as many as 3 to 6 months later. This relationship was more pronounced in younger children than in older adolescents. A practical interpretation is that if your child is young, it may be safest to not allow him or her to play violent video games.

In contrast, others argue against a direct relationship between gaming and aggression because there might be other variables contributing to the aggression.[30] The US Supreme Court ruled in 2011[31] that the evidence demonstrating a link between violent video games and aggression was not sufficiently convincing to limit these games. Thus, although you as a parent should be cautious about allowing your child (especially a young child) to play violent video games, the scientific evidence regarding its impact on aggressive behaviors remains inconclusive.

On the other end of the spectrum, some researchers have reported that some forms of gaming may be beneficial. The next chapter describes the potential positive effects of video games, and may help you better understand why your child likes to play them.

5

Can gaming be good for my child?

Your child probably started gaming when he was young, and you likely didn't see any harm in it then. It sure was easier to take a long car ride or to make it through a meal peacefully at a restaurant when he was occupied by a game. Some of the video games, at least the ones young kids play, are even educational. Some that older kids play also seem to have a cognitive or strategizing aspect, and that can't be all bad, right? If your child never excelled at sports, won't physical games like Wii help him get into better shape? Video games may be a good substitute for sports along other dimensions as well: like sports, they require regular practice in order to achieve goals and success. Is there anything wrong with kids practicing something to become good at it? Video games may also be fulfilling a social need—are your child's friends also gamers? Isn't having a set of gaming friends better than feeling alone?

Play and gaming

Your child may be getting some benefits from playing video games. By considering the possible positive effects, you may begin to understand what your child gains by playing at least some types of games in moderation.

Long before video games were invented, the famous psychologist Jean Piaget[1] suggested that play allows youth to create and practice with real-life situations. While playing, children design and test out responses to a variety of conditions. They experience their own reactions to their behaviors. They receive feedback based upon which of their actions make them feel happy, sad, amused, or confident. When playing interactively, children can also develop co-operative skills and feelings of social competence.

Everyone has observed young children playing, and it is difficult to imagine anyone objecting to play as a concept. As children grow up, traditional and highly accepted forms of play decrease. Toys and imaginary play are replaced by other forms, and video games are one of the most popular types of play activities in older children and adolescents.

Given the importance of play in general, gaming in moderation can certainly be considered normal. Gaming may even be associated with some positive effects.[2] So, exactly how is it that gaming can be a good thing for your child?

Social and psychological benefits

Research shows that playing nonviolent collaborative or helping video games is associated with increased "helping" behaviors in real life. For example, college students asked to play a collaborative and nonviolent game, such as Super Mario Sunshine or Chibi Robo, were more likely to help others in a task than those who played violent games.[3] Children who play more of these collaborative and non-violent games also have more positive social traits than children who do not play them.[4]

The most common games that kids develop problems with, how-ever, are not social games. You are probably not reading this book because you are worried about your child playing too many social or helping games! You are most likely concerned about your child playing aggressive or violent games.

Many online video games, although not replete with the kinds of social values most parents want to instill in their children, do have interpersonal dimensions. Most of the popular ones involve interactions with others through game-related personae. In virtual communities, players choose with whom they want to cooperate or help. They must also decide with whom they want to compete. It is possible that practicing these types of social skills online may generalize to improved relationships in the real world. For example, organizing and leading others to accomplish a common goal in a video game may nurture leadership abilities in real life. It may also enhance self-confidence. Children who do not have high levels of self-esteem can experience social competence when playing these games.

There may be other emotional benefits related to playing as well. Gaming may improve your child's mood. It may help him relax. When your child accomplishes a demanding feat in a game, he probably feels excited or elated. Games not only trigger positive emotional responses, but they can also evoke negative ones. You have, no doubt, seen your child get angry or frustrated and have an outburst during a game! The context of video games may make them safe environments in which your child can practice controlling these adverse emotions. Learning to regulate intense feelings, and especially strong negative emotions, is a skill very relevant to real life.

Video games also continuously provide new challenges to your child. They require that players be flexible and react quickly. In games like World of Warcraft, players need to be able to switch between avatars and adjust to environments that are changing constantly. Perseverative and rumination strategies block progress. Similarly, Portal 2 and other games of this genre involve solving intricate mazelike problems. Once an initial puzzle is solved, the rules alter, oftentimes dramatically. Switching thought strategies can frustrate players. They need to "unlearn" previous strategies to solve the new puzzle. Thus, some games encourage your child to practice new ways of managing emotions, including handling frustrations. The nature of online activities provides an anonymous environment in which your child can practice experiencing changes and the emotions that go along with them. This is not a bad thing!

Motivation, or persistence in tasks, is a key to success and achievement in real life, too. Kids who game excessively may appear unmotivated in terms of their education or work. One of the main complaints parents have about children who game a lot is that they are not applying themselves. However, while gaming, children do work toward goals. Video games provide constant and immediate acknowledgment of wins and losses. They present more challenging tasks once your child accomplishes simpler ones. Video games also provide intermittent rewards. These types of rewards are highly effective in both shaping and maintaining engagement. Continued play is rewarded, which motivates your child to keep playing. Although gaming may not enhance motivation to master schoolwork, the popularity of these games reflects their ability to motivate players to engage in them. If these experiences translate to persistence in other areas, your child may benefit practically from gaming.

In considering potential social and psychological benefits of gaming, you should remember that some gaming is "normal." Children who play video games for less than 1 hour a day appear to be more social than children who never play video games.[5] In other words, nonplayers might be *less* well adjusted than occasional players. Furthermore, low and moderate gaming is not associated with problems in any known area. Playing for over 3 hours a day, however, can be associated with difficulties, including reduced social behaviors and greater rates of depression.[6] If your child plays games in moderation and does not have problems related to playing, gaming is not harmful. It may even provide some emotional benefits.

Physical benefits

Playing active video games, such as Wii, may be physically beneficial.[7] Adolescents who play these active games are more likely to meet physical activity guidelines than those who do not.[8] Active gaming likely replaces sedentary screen time such as TV viewing and other Internet and nonactive gaming. However, the physical benefits are not pronounced, and most kids with gaming problems are not gaming excessively on the Wii!

Efforts are ongoing to use active gaming for medical rehabilitation in some people, such as those with multiple sclerosis.[9] To date, active gaming has caused improvements in overcoming some physical problems, but health effects are not pronounced or persistent.

Furthermore, any physical benefits relate solely to active gaming or Wii games. Other forms of gaming certainly do not improve physical fitness. To the contrary, time spent playing games on computers and other electronic devices is inversely related to overall physical activity levels.[10] In other words, the more that your child plays video games, the less likely he is to be physically active.

Cognitive benefits

Only active games hold the potential to increase physical activity levels, but gaming in other formats may enhance thought processes or cognition. Brain-training programs such as Lumosity have become popular in recent years, even though they are not designed as games per se or for entertainment. Developers claim that using their programs can enhance cognitive function. Some evidence suggests that these training packages may improve the specific cognitive abilities tapped by the tasks, but whether effects extend to real-world thinking and functioning is unclear.

Some argue that popular action video games may improve rapidity of response times, which may be important in some types of decision making.[11] One study[12] found players of action games such as Halo, Counterstrike, Gears of War, and Call of Duty had less activation in brain areas associated with attention than nonplayers. These results suggest that these gamers may direct attention more efficiently and filter out irrelevant information more effectively. However, it is possible that people who are drawn to play these games have less activation in these brain regions to begin with. In other words, game play may not have *led to* the changes.

Other forms of games, including puzzle games, do not appear to have much, if any, benefit for improving cognition.[13] The bulk of research shows it is unlikely that your child's cognition or thinking is improving by gaming in these genres.

Although playing popular video games does not seem to lead to meaningful cognitive improvements, games developed in the future might have more benefits. Efforts are ongoing to develop games for people with particular cognitive problems and those who need specific skills. Video games are being designed to assist older adults and individuals with brain damage[14] and to train physicians in technical surgery skills.[15] Similarly, educational tools are undergoing development to enhance learning generally. The goal is to directly target deficits in knowledge and skills. Eventually, electronic games and tools may enhance people's strengths, and correct their deficits, in a manner unparalleled with traditional learning. At the moment, however, your child is probably not gaining much cognitively from the games he is playing.

Exercising problem-solving skills, as encouraged by some video games, may be related to creativity.[16] In a real-word application of how gaming can be associated with creativity, researchers created an online game that modeled the genetic makeup of proteins and encouraged people around the world to play.[17] Top-scoring players generated solutions that allowed researchers to identify a crystal structure related to the AIDS virus. This solution had eluded AIDS researchers for years.

What all this means is that gaming is not an entirely "bad" behavior. Some types of games may lead to benefits, and some gaming is clearly normal. The positive aspects of playing video games, however, are best realized when it occurs in moderation. For people who have developed problems due to their gaming, the adverse consequences clearly outweigh any potential benefits.

INTERVENTION

6

Should I not worry about my child's gaming, or is it time to get professional help?

Pete is not sure whether his son, Sam, needs professional help. Sam is playing video games for multiple hours a day, and it is clearly interfering with their home life and his schoolwork. Pete is constantly arguing with his son about gaming, and it seems impossible to get him to go to bed at a decent hour, study for a test, or help with any household chores because of his excessive focus on gaming. Sam's mother, Amy, on the other hand, does not seem concerned enough about the situation. She has always been a pushover in Pete's mind, and she would allow Sam to do anything to avoid confrontation. She thinks Pete is being unreasonable in his approach toward their son's gaming and says all kids play as much or more than Sam. Pete took Sam to see a therapist a few years ago, when he and Amy got divorced. It seemed to help then. He is wondering if he should have Sam see a therapist again to help with the gaming.

A child who is gaming at a level that has caused any degree of harm can benefit from professional care or advice. Treatments can lead to improvements more rapidly when provided sooner, before problems become severe. Briefer and less intensive approaches can also be effective in these cases. The goal for you as a parent is to identify and correct troublesome behaviors and the problems they cause before they become significant. At the same time, you don't want to overreact to normal, nonproblematic gaming.

This chapter provides guidelines parents can use to recognize early problems with gaming. It also describes the types of treatments available for Internet gaming disorder. The last section of the chapter will help you decide whether you should seek professional care for your child. Regardless of whether or not your child needs professional help now, the information in this chapter is intended to provide a clear path for seeking assistance in the future if problems progress.

When to intervene: Distinguishing normal playing from problem playing

Chapter 3 outlined the nine symptoms of Internet gaming disorder. As Chapters 2 and 3 note, a relatively small proportion of kids, probably about 1.5%, have five or more symptoms of the disorder. A larger number experience just a few symptoms.

If your child has even one symptom, he is "at risk" for Internet gaming disorder. Certainly not every kid who is at risk will go on to develop more problems, but problems can progress over time and increase in severity. They can also remain stable or subside partially or completely.

The goal of *prevention* is to stop a condition from ever occurring in the first place. The intent of *treatment* is to reduce the severity of problems in those who already have experienced some difficulties. When problems are less intense, treatments can be brief and still effective. However, more severe problems usually require more intensive and prolonged treatments.

Frequency and duration

One simple method for identifying *possible* early problems with gaming in your child is to estimate the frequency and amount of time she spends gaming. If she rarely plays, she's unlikely to be experiencing negative consequences! Also keep in mind that some children play games regularly for long periods of time without any adverse effects. Most young people play video games, and the majority of them do so without developing any problems.

How long and how often your child games can help you determine whether gaming may be leading to problems. For example, in one study[1] children and adolescents who didn't have Internet gaming disorder typically played less than half the days in a week, and those with the disorder played 5 or more days per week. In terms of duration of play, nonproblem players gamed 12 hours a week on average. Although this is a substantial period of time, those with Internet gaming disorder played nearly twice as long—over 20 hours per week on average. These data provide ranges in which problems with game playing are likely to occur. Conservative estimates indicate that gaming 5 or more days a week and for over 12 hours a week *may* be associated with problems.

If your child is playing at or above these frequencies and intensities, then he or she may also be experiencing symptoms of Internet gaming disorder. Chapter 3 outlined these symptoms, and Worksheet 6.1 (located at the end of this chapter) provides a self-test for adolescents and adults based on these symptoms.[2] "Yes" responses indicate some problems have already occurred. If your child answers "yes" to between one and four items, he or she is at risk of developing Internet gaming disorder. If your child answers "yes" on five or more points, then he or she likely has Internet gaming disorder. This self-test is an informal assessment exercise and does not take the place of a diagnosis from a professional. However, if you see high scores, it is a good idea to have a professional assess your child.

For younger children who can't complete the questionnaire on their own, a parental version is in Worksheet 6.2 (also found at the end of this chapter). Again, if you notice any of these symptoms, your child may be at risk of developing Internet gaming disorder. The scoring system is the same as in Worksheet 6.1, and scores of 5 or more likely reflect Internet gaming disorder.

In summary, as a parent you should look for signs and symptoms of Internet gaming disorder in your child, especially if he or she is gaming daily or nearly every day and for more than 12 hours per week. You can use Worksheets 6.1 and/or 6.2 to assess whether your child has symptoms of Internet gaming disorder. If he has no or only a few difficulties, prevention of future problems will be the focus. The questionnaires in this chapter can also identify more significant problems. If your child has severe problems with gaming along with other mental health conditions, you may want to seek professional care in addition to instituting the steps the next chapters describe.

Professional care for Internet gaming disorder

Few people who could benefit from professional mental health services receive them. This situation is not unique to gaming. It is true of many mental health conditions, ranging from depression and anxiety to substance use disorders.

Reasons for not accessing services

In the case of other addictions like alcohol use disorders, less than half of adults with the condition ever seek treatment.[3] Among adolescents and young adults, the rates are even lower—under 10%. Those who do look for care tend to have more severe problems. For example, many people do not obtain treatment for alcohol use unless their (or their child's) drinking has come to the attention of their school or employer, or they have been arrested for impaired driving.

Adolescents and college students are particularly unlikely to obtain professional mental health care, and most who do are under pressure from parents or school administrators. Mandated treatment is the most common method by which students receive help for substance use problems. After attending a school function under the influence, for example, students may be required to participate in alcohol awareness programs. In contrast to substance use, however, playing video games is not illegal, and mandated treatment for Internet gaming disorder is unlikely.

Oftentimes people are hesitant to go to a mental health provider because they want to overcome the problem on their own.[4] Shame, stigma, and guilt all impact willingness to receive professional care, or even to seek informal assistance. Many parents of kids with addiction problems want to keep the issues within the family. They are embarrassed to have the problem out in the open. They may feel guilty themselves for whatever role they may feel they played in the process.

The good news is that guilt or shame, once recognized, can actually be helpful in solving the problem. In the next chapter on communication you will learn how to appraise your own current and past behaviors. You will also learn how to alter your responses to your child and take responsibility for mistakes you may feel you have made in the past. After reviewing this information and practicing new ways of responding to your child, you may feel you need more help or support in this process. If that is the case, you should certainly consider consulting a professional. Counselors' main roles relate to helping people cope with adverse situations. No matter whether the situation involves something entirely out of your control or something you may have played a role in unintentionally, counselors have seen and heard it all! Their job is not to judge you as a parent, but to help you and your child make the best of the current situation and grow from it. Seeking assistance is not a weakness, but a strength. It demonstrates your commitment to trying to improve the situation.

Although many parents feel some level of guilt related to their child's gaming problems, some are also hesitant to seek professional help because they feel that if their kid really wanted to stop, he could. Indeed, recovery from addiction without treatment *does* happen. About half of people with substance use and gambling disorders recover from them, and the majority do so without treatment.[5]

Similarly, some youth with Internet gaming disorder can recover from problems on their own.[6] Maturing out of addictions may be particularly relevant to adolescents and young adults. For example, drinking and substance use increase during adolescence. They peak at about 20 to 22 years of age, and thereafter steadily decline.[7] Similarly, gambling problems are common in late adolescence and early adulthood.[8] Once youth transition to adulthood, a sizeable proportion of those with prior problems overcome them.[9]

Although some children and young adults will outgrow their problems with gaming on their own, some will not. In fact, research to date indicates that over half of kids with Internet gaming problems will continue to have difficulties over the next 1 to 2 years at least. Thus, the safest recommendation is to intervene if your child is exhibiting problems, rather than taking a "wait and see" approach. The intervention can be professional, home-based, or both. As described next, the intensity and nature of assistance can be tailored to the severity of your child's problems. It can also be adjusted based on other conditions and symptoms your child may have.

Types of treatment for Internet gaming disorder

Treatment for addictions of all kinds can be broadly categorized into three groups: self-help communities, outpatient services, and inpatient/residential care. Each have their advantages and disadvantages.

Self-help communities. Self-help communities are available for free. Traditional self-help fellowships involve group meetings, and some urban areas have fellowships dedicated to Internet addiction. Even if no in-person groups are available in your community, there are self-help fellowships online. Online Gamers Anonymous (www.olganon.org) is a 12-step support and recovery organization for players and their loved ones. It offers discussion forums, online chats, and Skype meetings. Online sites should be used with caution, however, because they may have no professional staff monitoring communications. Some people find it counterintuitive, and potentially even dangerous, to recommend that a person with a problem related to Internet usage go online to find help and support. Nevertheless, this option may help some gamers.

Some parents also find online support services useful, but again it is important to recognize that nonprofessionals often design and manage these Internet-based forums. Many allow anyone to post messages, and some contain gamers' complaints about their families' attempts to minimize their gaming. You certainly may not find these online sites to be helpful! If reading blogs or posts about gaming problems troubles you, you should look for support elsewhere.

Psychotherapy and other outpatient services. Outpatient services are available through social workers, psychologists, and psychiatrists who provide treatment for many mental health problems. Generally, this treatment takes the form of psychotherapy, conducted alone with the individual who has gaming issues, or along with family members. Unfortunately, most mental health clinicians have never assisted patients with Internet gaming disorder, and those who have are unable to bill insurers for treatment of this condition. If your child has a psychiatric condition that is formally recognized by the American Psychiatric Association, the provider can treat and bill insurance for that other condition. Professional treatment for Internet gaming disorder alone is most often paid for out-of-pocket, and experienced providers are scarce in most areas due to how "new" the condition is.

A few specialized outpatient programs (meaning the individual attends the program daily or weekly but does not reside there) do offer treatment for Internet gaming disorder, here in the United States and elsewhere. As the next sections describe, most report that symptoms dissipate in many patients participating in these programs.

Although research on treatments of Internet gaming disorder is in its very early stages, a psychotherapeutic approach known as cognitive-behavioral therapy (CBT) appears useful,[10] and it is effective for other mental health conditions as well.[11] Briefly, CBT helps people identify the consequences of a behavior such as excessive gaming, both positive and negative. The positive effects your child may receive from gaming may include feeling connected to others and filling free time. The negative effects may relate to losing out on real-world friendships, not getting enough sleep, and doing poorly at school. CBT helps people better understand these consequences, teaching methods for coping with feelings and situations that put people at risk for the problem behavior. For example, loneliness may be a reason your child is gaming. Finding alternate methods to fulfill social needs may reduce loneliness and time spent gaming. If boredom puts your child at risk, then minimizing unstructured time should decrease gaming. A study that looked at people receiving CBT for Internet and gaming problems showed that most reduced their symptoms by the eighth session.[12] Chapters 7 to 9 outline how you can apply CBT techniques[13] with your own child, in your own home.

To access outpatient services, or to locate a psychotherapist who might be able to help address some of the issues causing problems for your family, talk to your primary care physician. He or she will be able to refer you to a provider in your community. Or, contact your health insurance company and ask for a list of mental health clinicians covered under your policy.

Inpatient/residential treatment. Although they are more common in Asian countries, inpatient and residential treatment programs for Internet addiction do exist in the United States. The most rigorous, lengthy, and costly of treatment approaches for Internet gaming disorder, these programs typically recommend stays of 30 days or longer, not unlike many substance addiction and eating disorder treatment programs. The best known is reSTART, an Internet Addiction Recovery Program in Fall City, Washington. This inpatient program institutes a total abstinence approach toward technology use for the first 45 to 90 days. It applies a variety of psychotherapeutic approaches in individual, group, and family formats. About 74% of patients who complete 45 or more days of treatment appear to have reductions in symptoms.[14]

Unfortunately, there are only a few clinics in North America that, like reSTART, specialize in treating gaming or Internet problems. It will be impractical and/or impossible for most people suffering from Internet gaming disorder to attend a residential treatment program far from home. Even for those who do desire assistance, entering these specialized treatment programs may not be possible logistically or financially; they tend to be extremely costly, and many of these programs do not accept insurance. The specialized programs often require direct payment for services, which can be in excess of tens of thousands of dollars.

Professional care for other psychiatric conditions

The most severe cases of Internet gaming disorder may require professional care (see also Chapter 11 on extreme cases). This is especially true for those who have other psychiatric conditions, such as depression, suicidality, anxiety, and ADHD. For kids and adults with extreme problems and distress, the recommendation is to seek professional help. Some people may benefit from medication. If psychotherapy and/or medication decrease other psychological concerns, it may then be easier to address the gaming.

Of notable concern is suicidality. If you are worried that your child is suicidal, you should immediately seek assistance. Signs or symptoms of suicidal behavior include:

- Making comments about being hopeless, helpless, or worthless
- Switching rapidly between being very sad and being very calm or happy
- Deep sadness, loss of interest in things, trouble sleeping and eating
- Frequently discussing death
- Making statements such as, "It would be better if I weren't here"

- Talking about suicide or discussing killing oneself
- Taking risks that could lead to death, such as driving too fast or running red lights
- Using drugs recklessly or stockpiling medications
- Giving away symbolic or important possessions
- Visiting or calling people to say goodbye

Risk is heightened if your child is exhibiting any of these signs and has attempted suicide in the past. You should call 911 if you think your child is in imminent danger. Alternatively, you can contact a suicide hotline to discuss your concerns. They will help assess the situation and refer you for assistance in your area.

For depression, anxiety, ADHD, and other mental illnesses, you can speak with a physician or your child's pediatrician, or anonymously with a mental health hotline. Even if your child has no medical insurance, there are services available for free or on sliding-scale fee. You may need to ask specifically for such assistance, but many hospitals and clinics do provide it.

If your older adolescent or adult child is reluctant or refuses professional care, you can try to encourage him or her to attend a onetime assessment. After an evaluation, your child may be more open to discussing options. Often, meeting initially with a trusted family physician may be perceived as less stigmatizing than meeting with a psychiatrist or other mental health professional. Although not all family care physicians are experienced in diagnosing mental health conditions, they can serve as an initial contact. They should be able to refer to specialized providers when necessary.

Professional treatment is recommended for other psychiatric conditions, such as depression, anxiety, ADHD, and social phobia. Most clinicians experienced in treating these conditions will not have experience with Internet gaming disorder, but the techniques described in subsequent chapters can be delivered along with professional care if other serious mental health problems exist. They can also be provided on their own when gaming is the sole or primary concern.

Worksheet 6.1
Gaming experiences self-test

Please circle "yes" or "no" in response to each question. "Gaming" means playing any electronic or video game. These can be played on computers, iPads, iPhones, Androids, Nintendo, Xbox, PlayStation, Wii, etc.

In the past year,		
1a. Did you often think about gaming, even when you were doing other things?	No	Yes
1b. Did you spend a lot of time planning when you can game next?	No	Yes
2a. Did you feel restless, worried, angry, or sad when you tried to stop gaming for several days?	No	Yes
2b. Did you feel restless, worried, angry, or sad when you could not game for a couple of days in a row?	No	Yes
3a. Did you game longer than you used to, and still not feel excited or satisfied by it?	No	Yes
3b. Did you feel gaming was becoming a more and more important part of your life?	No	Yes
4a. Did you try to stop or cut down how much you game, but fail in your attempts?	No	Yes
4b. Did you feel you could not control how much time you spent gaming?	No	Yes
5a. Did you cut down a lot on other hobbies or activities because of how much you were gaming?	No	Yes
5b. Did you decrease time spent with friends or family a lot because of how much you were gaming?	No	Yes
6a. Did you often not get enough sleep because you were gaming?	No	Yes

	No	Yes
6b. Were you often late to school or work because you were gaming?	No	Yes
6c. Did you often spend too much money on games?	No	Yes
6d. Did you often argue with your parents or others about how much you game?	No	Yes
6e. Did you often not do important household chores because you were gaming?	No	Yes
6f. Did you often not do homework or work projects because you were gaming?	No	Yes
7a. Did you often lie about how much you game?	No	Yes
7b. Did you regularly try to keep others from knowing about how much you game?	No	Yes
8a. Did you game to escape or forget about real-life problems?	No	Yes
8b. Did you game more when other things in your life were not going well?	No	Yes
9a. Did you risk or lose a relationship because of gaming?	No	Yes
9b. Did you risk or lose an opportunity at school or work because of gaming?	No	Yes
9c. Did you skip school or work because you were gaming?	No	Yes

Scoring: A response of "Yes" to one or more items within each number (or boxed section) results in one point to the score. For example, responding "Yes" to item 1a or item 1b results in 1 point; a "Yes" response to both 1a and 1b also results in 1 point. Similarly, a "Yes" response to one or more of items 6a through 6f leads to 1 point, but you cannot get more than one point for the items labeled with the number 6.

Scores range from 0 to 9. Scores of 5 or higher indicate possible Internet gaming disorder.

Worksheet 6.2
Parent questionnaire for child's gaming problems

Please circle "yes" or "no" in response to each question. "Gaming" means playing any electronic or video game. These can be played on computers, iPads, iPhones, Androids, Nintendo, Xbox, PlayStation, Wii, etc.

In the past year,		
1a. Did your child often talk about gaming, even when he or she was not gaming?	No	Yes
1b. Did your child often rush off to game, even when he or she was involved in other activities?	No	Yes
2a. Did your child act restless, worried, angry, or sad when he or she could not game for a few days in a row? (Note: Do not include times that you would not allow him or her to play.)	No	Yes
3a. Did your child game a lot longer than he or she used to?	No	Yes
3b. Did gaming seem to be the most important part of your child's life?	No	Yes
4a. Did your child express an interest in trying to cut down or stop gaming?	No	Yes
5a. Did your child substantially reduce time on other hobbies or activities because of gaming?	No	Yes
5b. Did your child spend a lot less time with friends or family because of gaming?	No	Yes
6a. Did your child often not get enough sleep because he or she was gaming?	No	Yes
6b. Was your child often late to school because he or she was gaming?	No	Yes

6c. Did your child often spend too much money on games?	No	Yes
6d. Did you often argue with your child about how much he or she games?	No	Yes
6e. Did your child often not do important household chores because he or she was gaming?	No	Yes
6f. Did your child often not do homework because he or she was gaming?	No	Yes
7a. Did your child often lie about how much he or she was gaming?	No	Yes
7b. Did your child regularly try to keep you or others from knowing about how much he or she was gaming?	No	Yes
8a. Did your child appear to game more often after having a bad day at school, or after experiencing a bad event?	No	Yes
9a. Did your child risk or lose a friendship because of gaming?	No	Yes
9b. Did your child risk or lose an opportunity at school because of gaming?	No	Yes
9c. Did your child skip school because of gaming?	No	Yes

Scoring: A response of "Yes" to one or more items within each number (or boxed section) results in one point to the score. For example, responding "Yes" to item 1a or item 1b results in 1 point; a "Yes" response to both 1a and 1b also results in 1 point. Similarly, a "Yes" response to one or more of items 6a through 6f leads to 1 point, but you cannot get more than one point for the items labeled with the number 6. Scores range from 0 to 9.

Scores of 5 or higher indicate possible Internet gaming disorder.

7

Gaming, communication, and your child

*Pete is a father who likes rules and order. He has little tolerance for
digressions or considering other perspectives. He wants things done
and done right. His ex-wife, Amy, on the other hand, lets people,
including their son, walk all over her (he believes). She would rather
say nothing than confront a situation. Yet, she is the one who gets
emotional and cries when things don't go the way she wants. Their
different parenting styles, and personalities, have long been a source
of contention and played a role in their divorce. They now share
custody of their teenage son, Sam, who Pete thinks has a gaming
problem. Amy agrees that their son plays far too much and that it
is impacting his grades at school, but she doesn't seem to want to do
much about it. Pete believes Amy is the main source of the gaming
problem. Amy thinks the problem originated with Pete.*

You play an important role in your child's life, and you can influence
your child's behavior, including his or her gaming. You will be able
to modify your child's behavior most effectively if your actions and
words are positive and supportive, and if your child perceives them
as such. By closely evaluating your own attitudes and behaviors toward gaming and how you respond to your child, you may be in a
better position to help him or her—as well as yourself—deal with a
difficult situation.

In this chapter, you will learn about how you respond to your
child, both positively and negatively. Some aspects of these exercises

may be hard to consider honestly, because you may be feeling angry, hurt, or worried. These are common reactions and concerns. Remember, however, that an upfront appraisal of the situation is best. Covering up or denying issues will never resolve them. Additionally, do not expect that the situation will dissipate quickly or that your relationship with your child will change overnight, even if you take all the recommendations to heart. Your child's gaming problems have evolved over time, and they will take time to resolve. Similarly, your relationship with your child has developed throughout his or her lifetime, and it, too, will take time to improve.

Methods of responding to gaming

Let's first assess your current pattern of responding to your child's gaming.[1] It is important to identify anything you may be doing, intentionally or unintentionally, that may serve to punish or control your child. Your child may end up avoiding or resenting you if you rely primarily on negative or punishing behaviors. These behaviors can provoke him or her to react negatively and even to game more.

The top section of Worksheet 7.1 lists reactions some parents have toward gaming. Check any that you identify with. Try to be honest with yourself as you review the checklist. Even if your intentions are good, you may be responding in ways that your child perceives as negative, especially when you are feeling frustrated.

For all the reactions toward gaming you checked off at the top of Worksheet 7.1, consider how they made you feel at the time. Think about how you felt immediately after engaging in that behavior. Also think about how those incidents make you feel now, even if it is years later.

The responses in Worksheet 7.1 generally leave everyone involved feeling mad or hurt—including you. When you are trying everything you can to reduce problems with your child, yet nothing seems to be working, you get more desperate in your attempts to stop his or her behaviors.

Worksheet 7.1
Reactions to video game playing

Check the reactions you have had to video game playing.

- ☐ *Ignoring the gaming because it is easier than getting into an argument about it*
- ☐ *Playing video games yourself (with or without your child)*
- ☐ *Congratulating attainment of scores and statuses*
- ☐ *Explaining, justifying, or making excuses (e.g., all kids play these games; my child is really no different; playing video games is better than drinking or doing drugs)*
- ☐ *Protecting your child's image (e.g., concealing playing from other family members or friends, or defending him/her when others criticize or tease)*
- ☐ *Expressing disapproval*
- ☐ *Coaxing or pleading*
- ☐ *Crying*
- ☐ *Nagging*
- ☐ *Lecturing*
- ☐ *Becoming angry, yelling, or screaming*
- ☐ *Making threats or ultimatums*
- ☐ *Making sarcastic remarks*
- ☐ *Bartering (e.g., "If you stop playing, then I'll _____," or "If you don't stop, then I'll _____.")*
- ☐ *Punishing*
- ☐ *Trying to "get even" (e.g., doing something your child dislikes because s/he is spending so much time playing games)*
- ☐ *Paying for gaming, such as for cell phone bills, Internet access, or gaming subscriptions*
- ☐ *Taking care of your child's responsibilities (e.g., doing homework or housework s/he should have done, paying for things s/he should pay for, waking him/her up for school)*
- ☐ *Calling in sick to school or work for your child*
- ☐ *Other:*_____

_____

_____

_____

_____

After assessing how your reactions affect you, consider how they impact your child and the gaming behaviors. Do they make your child angry? Or, does your child simply withdraw from you when you try to intervene?

You probably realize that your attempts are ineffective in changing your child's gaming behaviors. Importantly, if the gaming has not stopped or reduced in the past in response to the behaviors you checked, it is unlikely that it will slow or cease in response to them in the future.

Have any of the behaviors you checked in Worksheet 7.1 ever been successful in decreasing gaming? If the answer to that question is "no" or "rarely," you may be ready to try new methods. The remainder of the exercises in this chapter will help you identify communication styles that are troublesome as well as ones that can be helpful—for both you and your child.

Identify behaviors that allow gaming

Take some time to consider whether you are reacting to gaming in some ways that might encourage it unintentionally. Even though you clearly do not intend to promote gaming, your actions, words, and even failure to act at times can provide your son or daughter with reasons to continue playing. You probably have shielded your child from experiencing negative consequences of excessive gaming. The concepts of denial, enabling, and bailouts are common in addictions. They apply to excessive gaming as well.

Denial

Simply put, denial is refusing to believe that something is true. In psychology, it refers to keeping unpleasant realities from conscious awareness. It's a defense mechanism.

You may feel that your child is in denial about his or her problems with gaming. Your child may not recognize or admit to problems that his or her behaviors are causing. Denial arises in part because your child does not want to stop gaming.

Denial can go both ways. Your child may deny difficulties with gaming, and you may also deny any role you are playing in the situation. You may not be denying that your child has a problem with gaming, but you may be in denial concerning some of the conditions that led to it. Pete would probably deny any role he may have played in his son's excessive gaming, but it is likely that aspects of his parenting style contributed to the problem. If you or other family members are also gamers, you may feel ambivalence related to the role gaming plays in your lives. You or your partner may enjoy gaming and be able to control it, but your son cannot seem to. By allowing gaming in your home, are you contributing to the problem? By learning to pay better attention to how you respond to your child's gaming, you can reduce your own denial. And, by minimizing your denial, you can help your child—and yourself—cope better.

Enabling

To *enable* is to provide someone with the means or opportunity to do something. Enabling may be indirect and relate to failing to set appropriate boundaries. It may also be direct and involve providing money or goods to continue a behavior.

You might be enabling gaming by allowing devices that facilitate it in your home. For younger children and especially for gaming with specific devices (e.g., Nintendo, Xboxes), the simplest solution is to take away the game-playing devices or remove them from your home entirely. You could throw them away or donate them to a library, school, or community center.

Many parents think this is an extreme suggestion, as do most children! You may have paid a great deal of money for the device.

You, your child, or other family members likely invested in a lot of games for it. Throwing it out is like throwing money down the drain. In some cases, your child may have purchased the device with his or her own money, and giving it away may be tantamount to stealing it. Some devices, such as phones, tablets, and personal computers, are used for purposes beyond gaming. Throwing them away would eliminate the ability to use the devices for schoolwork or communication.

Although all these rationalizations may be true, allowing continued access to gaming devices is enabling your child's use. Admitting to the enabling is an important step toward achieving and maintaining more control over the situation. If you have a young child, it is easier to consider complete removal of the device. Throwing out gaming devices is a clear sign that gaming will no longer be condoned in the home. Although this action will surely be met with a great deal of resistance, it is an option for parents who have tried unsuccessfully to reduce gaming by other methods. Chapter 11 describes how to remove gaming devices from your home and tips for putting a temporary or permanent ban on them.

If you have an older adolescent or an adult child with a gaming problem, you may be less inclined to eliminate gaming devices. Nevertheless, you can discontinue any financial (and emotional) support you may be providing for their use. Pete, in our example, may have purchased a laptop for his son and pays for the Internet service that allows for gaming on it. He may need to greatly restrict its use (i.e., just for schoolwork) to stop the gaming.

Later in this chapter you will encounter information on how to follow through with the resolve to no longer enable gaming once you recognize the choices over which you have control.

Bailouts

Another type of behavior that allows gaming to continue, one that is often more extreme in nature than enabling, is a bailout.

Bailouts include allowing a child to stay home "sick" from school after spending a long night playing, or covering up for him when he avoids social, school, or work responsibilities. Pete may have been embarrassed to let his son go to school after he was up all night gaming; he preferred to let him stay home rather than fail the test he didn't study for. If you pay for your adult child's cell phone bill because he doesn't earn enough money to do so himself, you are, in essence, bailing him out of his financial responsibilities, as well as enabling his gaming on it. When you recognize how you may be allowing gaming to continue unhampered, you can stop your own behaviors that are contributing to your child's gaming problems.

Many parents support gaming, although this support is often unintentional. Once they recognize how their behaviors impact their child, they can alter them. When your child can no longer rely on you to support his gaming, he may be more ready to stop it.

Return to Worksheet 7.1, and check any additional ways in which you may have enabled your child to game or bailed him out of situations that arose from his gaming. Add specific examples of times or situations in which you may have used denial, enabling, or bailout strategies in the "other" section.

Interfering with natural consequences

The primary reason people play video games is because they enjoy them and find them fun. A reason people *stop* a behavior is because they experienced, directly or indirectly, a serious consequence from it. When this consequence is extreme, it is referred to as reaching "rock bottom." Rock bottom means actually having encountered a substantive problem, perhaps even a seemingly insurmountable one. These are the natural effects that eventually arise from addictive behaviors. In some cases, they may take decades to occur. In others, rock bottom can come suddenly and quickly.

Although no one ever wants their child or loved one to reach rock bottom, experiencing negative consequences is what often tips the scales in favor of ceasing or reducing a problem behavior. As noted in Chapter 6, most people with addictive behaviors never seek or receive treatment, and those who do typically do so after having encountered a significant issue because of their behavior. Sometimes a big scare is enough to trigger change.

Because the negative consequences of excessive gaming can ultimately lead your child to stop this behavior, it is critical that you become aware of how you may be preventing your child from experiencing them. In many cases, the issue may be relatively minor, such as oversleeping due to late-night gaming. However, even if you are doing something as seemingly harmless as waking your child up for school in the morning after she was up late gaming, you are in fact condoning her late-night gaming episodes. You are enabling that behavior.

By no longer interfering with gaming's adverse effects, you will demonstrate to your child that you are serious about changing your ways of dealing with it. Your behaviors, in turn, will help her evaluate the pros and cons of continuing excessive gaming. Once you stop enabling, your child will have to take greater personal responsibility for her own behavior.

There are four steps to take in order to best prepare yourself to allow your child to experience the natural, negative consequences of gaming.

Step 1: First, select a situation in which you had been unknowingly or unintentionally supporting gaming. For example, you may have engaged in a conversation with your child about how well he did in one of his games, or you may have purchased a game console for him as a gift. You may think of similar situations off the top of your head. You may also want to return to the behaviors you checked in Worksheet 7.1.

Step 2: Once you have a specific denial, enabling, or bailout example in mind, think about what the consequences might have been had you not enabled gaming in that situation. Even seemingly benign situations are worth consideration. For example, you may have displayed excitement for your child when he announced a status he achieved in a game. Think about what would have happened had you NOT engaged in that discussion. Would your son have felt unsupported? Would he have felt that you were disinterested in him? How would you have felt if you did not talk with him about the game he was playing? Would you have felt like a bad parent? Would you have felt as though you were being unsupportive? Were you just glad he was talking with you about anything, even if it was just a video game?

Step 3: Now, explore potential problems with not supporting gaming in that situation or manner. What difficulties may have arisen if you had not taken part in a conversation about one of your son's games? Do you think he would be less likely to start another discussion with you in the future? Would he have gone right back to the computer to play more if you didn't discuss his high score with him? Or, might he have tried to get your attention in some other way?

Step 4: Finally, think about other directions in which that situation could have gone. For example, if your son told you he was excited about accomplishing a really difficult mission in League of Legends, you could have inquired about whether there are other things he would like to be achieving. If he used to play a sport and is no longer playing it, you may have commented, "I remember how happy you used to be when you scored a goal, or your team won an important game. Do you ever miss playing soccer? Have you seen your old friend from the team lately?" This discussion, while not completely dismissing his enthusiasm, brings the topic back to other positive achievements and good memories of a healthier pastime than gaming. You could decide that you are no longer going to discuss his games with him and simply change the topic to something else when he talks about his playing.

Now that we've reviewed these four steps for preparing to allow your child to experience the natural, negative effects of his gaming, let's consider an example. Perhaps you purchased a Nintendo for your child, and now he is playing it for hours every day. Think about how that birthday or celebration may have gone had you not purchased the Nintendo. Would your child have been angry with you if you had given him something else instead?

If you cannot bring yourself to get rid of the Nintendo, you may make a resolution to purchase no more games or gaming devices. When this one breaks or becomes outdated, you will not replace it. You will talk with your partner (or your child's other parent figure, if applicable) to make sure he or she is on board with this decision too, to ensure a unified approach.

In these cases, the natural consequences of the enabling behavior were somewhat minimal. Other more substantial negative effects may have also occurred from excessive gaming. For example, if you have been covering for your adult child to stay home "sick" from work when you know he has been up all night gaming, you probably recognize that missing work may have dire consequences for his job. He may even be fired. Although no one wants their child to lose a job, this can be a natural consequence of excessive gaming. Experiencing such an extreme consequence may be what your child needs to accept responsibility for his behaviors. If your child loses a job now, that may be better than continued excessive gaming, which ultimately could lead to even more extreme negative effects down the road.

You may need assistance to carry out changes. You may need to talk with your partner and other family members to ensure they don't cover for your child and say he is sick if the boss calls the home phone number. Pete may need to make sure that Amy is on board with not allowing Sam to stay home from school even if he didn't complete his homework or study for a test. In the example above, you may need to encourage family members to not bring up gaming or not engage in discussions about video games. If you have other children, and your son with the gaming problem attempts to discuss a game at dinner, quickly turn your attention to your other children and ask them about their accomplishments. Diverting the attention to others will likely end the focus on gaming.

A common issue for parents relates to paying for their child's cell phone or home Internet connections, both of which can also be used for gaming. If you pay for gaming indirectly via these systems, you may want to consider what discontinuing that financial assistance will mean. Although your child may resent that you are no longer paying his phone bill or funding his smartphone, a non-smartphone option may reduce the gaming. Cell phones without data plans or Wi-Fi connections can still make calls and texts. If your child has to get a part-time job to regain use of a smartphone, he will have less time to play.

Clearly, removing home Internet use is a measure of last resort, and not one to be considered lightly. If, after reading this book, you decide that the only way to stop excessive gaming is to cancel your Internet service, others in the family will also no longer be able to use the Internet at home. You could consider a password-protected line without disclosing the password. However, if you choose to cancel your Internet service, your child will be less likely to see the change as a punishment and more likely to see it as a move your entire family is taking together, if everyone in the home is subject to the same expectations. If the gamer is being singled out, he will be more resentful than if it is a family decision to go Internet free (temporarily or permanently; see Chapter 11) because of the problems it has created within the family.

If you do decide to remove the Internet from your home, be prepared for your child to protest greatly. He may shout at you, say he hates you, and bring up examples of what a bad parent you are. It is important to not back down. You can remind your child that the reason you are discontinuing the Internet is because you love him and you are doing everything you can, even something that will greatly inconvenience you, to help him overcome problems with gaming. You child may deny problems with gaming and become desperate; he may even threaten to leave home. If he does, you can remind him that there is not only no Internet on the streets, there is also no food or shelter. You plan to continue providing them for him. You could even discuss how savings from the Internet can be directed toward other fun things from which your child and the whole family can benefit. If he threatens to go to another relative's home, inform him that you have already discussed the plan with them and that they too will block his use of the Internet if he moves in with them. If your child says he's going to stay with a friend, you may need to contact that friend's parents to explain the situation.

If you are worried that your child may be suicidal, talk to a professional about how to intervene rather than giving in regarding Internet use (see Chapter 6). Remember that if your child is desperate enough to threaten suicide, the problem is far worse than gaming alone—restoring the Internet will not solve anything at this point, and will only cover up the issues your child is having.

Most parents won't need to go to the extent of removing the Internet entirely from the home. Usually, less drastic approaches can solve the problem. Whatever changes you ultimately decide to make, however, will require a change in how you approach gaming and Internet use more generally with your child. As you make decisions while reading this and the next few chapters, practice how you will explain your decision about no longer supporting or interfering with the natural consequences of excessive gaming. Be supportive, firm, and nonconfrontational. Avoid getting angry or accusatory. Remember that the goal is to no longer support the gaming in any way. You are simply allowing the natural consequences of excessive gaming to occur if it persists.

Consider John, a father who knows his daughter is up all night playing video games. He is aware that he is enabling her by waking her up for school each day. He does not want her to be late or miss school, so it just seems easier to keep waking her up. John reflects upon the following issues.

> **Situation:** *My child is up until all hours playing video games. She never gets up for school on her own.*

> **Typical response:** *I always wake her, which is getting more and more difficult.*

Possible alternative response: *I could institute a 10 p.m. ban on computers and all electronics that feature video games and quit waking her up.*

Possible problems: *My child will resent my taking the electronics away in the evenings. And, if I don't wake her up she might not get up at all. She'll oversleep and be late for school. I could even get in trouble for having a delinquent child.*

Solution: *I know I am responsible for getting her to school, but I also need to take responsibility to ensure she is not playing games all night. I could say to her, "I know that you are used to my waking you up for school in the morning, but I'm not going to do that anymore. For the next month, I am taking your computer, the Nintendo, and all the smartphones and the iPad at 10 p.m., before I go to bed. I will keep them in my bedroom at night. This means you will need to finish all your homework before 10 p.m. I also bought you an alarm clock to help you get up on time, which I think you will be able to do easily if you are not gaming after 10 p.m. and get your homework completed earlier. If you don't get up in time for school on your own or if you are playing video games after 10 p.m. any day over the next 4 weeks, then I will give away the Nintendo and stop service on your smartphone. I will also password protect your computer and the iPad so that you can only turn them on while I am watching. I understand that you will not like this plan, but it is necessary for us both to make some changes. If you do get up on your own for school each day and if you are not playing any video games after 10 p.m., we can reconsider these rules in 1 month."*

In this example, John keeps calm and matter-of-fact. As hard as this plan may be to follow through with, it is a good solution for ending the enabling behavior of allowing his child to play games throughout the night and waking her up every morning.

Worksheet 7.2 outlines a couple of additional examples. Use this worksheet to consider at least two or three different specific situations in which you have been enabling game-playing behavior. Think about an alternate response that does not involve denial,

Worksheet 7.2
Typical and alternate reactions to gaming behaviors

Situation	Typical response	Possible alternate response	Possible problems	Solution
Example: My son is excited about a game or his status.	I congratulate him (because I'm happy he's talking to me).	I could quickly move the conversation to another topic.	He may feel unsupported. He may not want to talk about anything.	I could talk about his accomplishments in other areas.
Example: He plays when he should be doing homework.	I sometimes ignore it (because I don't want to argue).	I could ask him to show me homework. I can remind him no play until homework is completed.	He will get angry, or tell me he has no homework today.	I can ask teachers to email me assignments. I will take away the computer for the day if he plays before homework.

Situation	Typical response	Possible alternate response	Possible problems	Solution

enabling, or bailouts. Consider the possible difficulties that may arise if you prevent the gaming from continuing. Determine a solution to the situation, and describe a method to explain your actions to your child. If you need to discuss plans with your partner or other family members, consider how you will do that as well.

Finally, review your explanations for ceasing denial, enabling, and bailouts, as well as for any direct or indirect support you may be providing for gaming. Are your solutions realistic? Do you need to involve anyone else in carrying out the plan? How is your child likely to respond to your new solution to the situation? Are there additional ways you could describe your actions? Are there other things you can do that will achieve the same effect, while minimizing defensiveness?

As you consider your own reactions to your child's gaming, be sure to give yourself credit! By completing the worksheets in this chapter and reflecting upon your own role in the gaming problem, you are actively making strides toward a better relationship with your child. Don't continue feeling guilty about the past. Instead, focus your energies on the positive changes you are making now.

The next section describes communication styles. After reviewing it, you may alter some of your initial reactions to these situations. You may also uncover more effective ways of talking with your child.

Communication styles

In reviewing your typical—and now new—patterns of responding to gaming behaviors, it is helpful to consider what psychologists have identified as the three basic interpersonal response styles: aggressive, passive, and assertive. Everyone uses all three styles from time to time, and there are some situations in which passive or even aggressive styles may be appropriate. However, the goal for helping your child, and at the same time for helping yourself, is to practice assertive responses while minimizing aggressive and passive ones. If you typically use aggressive or passive response patterns, recognizing instances in which you use them and considering other more assertive styles may assist both of you.

Passive response

A *passive* response is one in which the problem is ignored, or the individual accepts responsibility inappropriately. A passive response may involve not even acknowledging that your child remained glued to the computer screen all afternoon. It may also include not discussing poor grades at school that likely resulted at least in part from excessive gaming. It may involve guilt on your part. As a parent you may accept blame for your child's gaming because you feel that you were not always there when your child needed you, or you weren't able to give him enough attention. Think about your own passive responses to game playing. Consider how it made you feel when you responded passively.

Aggressive response

An *aggressive* response is one in which an individual attempts to belittle or overpower another. For example, Pete may say to his teenage son, "I'm sick and tired of you wasting your life on those stupid games. I've had it. So long as you live under my roof, you will follow my rules. No more playing these games, and I mean it!"

Try to recall some aggressive responses you have had to gaming. If you have ever used statements like the one above, put yourself in your child's shoes and imagine how he feels when he hears you say them. Do you think it makes him want to stop playing? Or, do you think it may make him reactive and want to play more out of defiance? Do you think he would see his own behavior as contributing to the problem, or do these kinds of remarks make you seem unreasonable? Would you want to spend more time with someone who spoke to you in that manner? Did your parents speak to you like that, and if so, how did it make you feel? By experiencing reactions from your child's perspective, you may gain new insight into your relationship.

Assertive response

Now, consider an *assertive* response. An assertive response states the issue simply and objectively, and it provides potential solutions to prevent the problem from recurring. For example, upon coming home after a long day at work, a parent may say, "I see you've started playing video games today. I'm sorry I got home so late. I had a big problem at work today and had to stay late. Next time, I'll call you to let you know when I have to stay long at work, and you can make dinner on those days. When I can't get home on time, I'd really appreciate your helping out with some of the household responsibilities, and that way we can both have a nice dinner. What should we get at the store that you want to try making next time that I'm late?"

This response is less likely to alienate the teenager. It places some of the responsibility on the parent because she or he was not home. It also provides a solution for not repeating the behavior in the future. Not only will the parent call, but the parent will also place a clear expectation on the child in terms of making dinner. By allowing the child a choice in the decision (what she or he would like to make), the parent will increase the probability that the child will engage in the intended behavior (making dinner). Finally, this response also incorporates an alternate activity (preparing a meal the child chooses and likes) in place of a typical gaming time (when the parent is not home). A precommitment is also included, and the child is asked to commit to preparing dinner the next time the parent has a late night at work. Imagine how your child may respond to such a remark the next time you arrive home and find him gaming.

Assertiveness is important because it can help *you respond differently to your child's gaming behaviors.* These skills should assist you with speaking up when necessary. Assertive behavior can prevent you from hurting your child's feelings or getting into arguments. Practicing assertiveness should help you be more effective in communicating in general. By being assertive, you will also feel more in control and you will feel more confident.

Importantly, assertiveness skills may also *help your child reduce gaming*. When you handle interpersonal situations more effectively, your child will notice the change. Some kids with gaming problems play after arguments; others play to avoid anxiety-provoking interactions or to recover from them. Practicing assertiveness skills will ensure that your interactions with your son or daughter become more positive in nature. You will manage difficult situations effectively and feel good about doing so. Your child will also feel more positive about interacting with you. Your child will no longer be playing games to cope with negative feelings about adverse interactions with you. When you use assertive communication, you both win!

Tips for assertive communication

Not every situation will go perfectly, and not every time will you remember to act assertively. However, the more you practice acting assertively, the more natural it will become. Recognizing when you failed to act assertively will also help you respond differently the next time a similar situation arises.

The following ten tips will help you respond assertively in a range of situations. Common examples of aggressive or passive responses are also described, along with how they can be reframed assertively.

1. Be brief, yet specific and clear. A lengthy discussion will rarely go as planned. If your child is gaming when he should not be, there is no reason to address anything beyond the current situation at that point in time. A long conversation may also muddle the meaning or your intent. Rather than engaging in an extensive conversation about everything that you feel is going wrong, simply point out what needs to happen now, clearly. An example is, "Max, I need you to turn off that game right now."

2. Be positive. No one enjoys hearing negatives. If you can frame a situation in the positive, your child will receive it better. Rather than stating, "Max, those games are a waste of your time," you would be better off with, "Max, I need you to turn off that game right now so we can all have dinner together. I have some news to share, and I want to hear about your day too."

3. Use "I" statements and label your own needs or feelings. Tell your child what you desire. Be specific about what you want and any changes that you request. For example, an assertive response is, "I would feel better if you talked to me when I came home from work. Even if it is only for a minute, I just like to know how your day went." In contrast, a common aggressive response is, "You don't even bother talking to me any more you're so wrapped up in those games."

Relatedly, try not to use "you" statements. Examples are, "You don't seem to care about anything anymore," and "You never talk with me like you used to." Making statements with "you" in them usually causes the other person to act defensively and strike back.

4. State why you want it. Instead of saying, "I don't like how much time you spend playing games," say, "It really worries me when you spend so much time playing games when I know you have a lot of homework to finish."

5. Acknowledge your child's rights and feelings. Consider the statement, "I know you are in the middle of a game, but it is time to come to dinner now. In the future, it would be best if you set an alarm or timer so you end your game at a convenient time for you, but before 6 p.m., when we eat." That remark is more likely to make both you and your child feel better than if you were to say, "Those games are just a waste of time, and you don't even bother eating dinner with the family because you are so busy playing them."

6. Balance the negative with the positive. If you have to be critical or say something that implies blame, express something positive first. For example, "I know you really enjoy playing games on the computer. However, lately, I feel like you are not doing your homework or picking up your room like you used to."

7. Offer to help. When possible and appropriate (i.e., not in the context of enabling), offer assistance. For example, "I'm going to do laundry right after dinner, so if your clothes are ready, I can stick them in with the rest of the wash." This statement is brief, specific, clear, and positive, and it offers to assist, but it does not enable the child (presuming that the parent usually washes the child's clothes). Even if the parent does not, the child must complete his share of the agreement—to stop gaming at least long enough to clean up his room—to benefit from the assistance. By comparison, a more passive response would be, "Could you try to clean up your room sometime?"

8. Speak firmly. Your message should be said with authority, but not hostility. A statement like, "I don't really think that you should be spending so much time playing games on your iPhone," is a passive response. In contrast, an assertive response is, "I know I cannot control what you do, but I will no longer be paying for your iPhone bill anymore because I don't want to be supporting gaming on it. I have paid the penalty for early termination of the Internet plan on your phone. If you want to start a new service, you will need to pay for it with your own money. I will keep paying for you to be able to send and receive calls and text messages, though, because I don't want you to be without a phone at school."

9. Respond promptly. Rapid responses convey to the other person that you are sure of yourself. Do not wait for several hours or until the next day to confront a situation or make a request. If your child is not following rules related to gaming, it needs to be addressed as soon as you notice it. For example, you may go into your son's room and state, "The computer needs to stay in the living room, and as we discussed you are not to play games on it on school nights. Please either give it to me, or bring it into the living room yourself right now."

10. Deliver a consistent message. Your body gestures and facial expressions should relate to your message. Look at your child when you speak and when you listen. Good nonverbal communication promotes the impression that you are serious about your message. You cannot be assertive if you are crying or if you have an angry scowl on your face. Relatedly, keep rules and regulations about gaming consistent. You cannot expect your child to abide by rules if you are constantly changing them, or if you are inconsistently monitoring and applying them. The next chapter describes how you can decide upon appropriate rules for gaming.

Relatedly, once you have rules for your child's electronic usage, be sure to apply similar rules to yourself. Although you may not be playing video games on your smartphone, many parents constantly check texts, emails, or social media while they are with their children. If you want your child to begin living a more screenfree life, then your behaviors should be consistent with your desires for your child. Begin to think about how you can communicate more effectively by examining examples of how you may be adding to the communication problem. This may include reducing your own "screen time."

In considering your verbal responses to your child, replace examples of aggressive and passive responding with a more effective approach using the suggestions above. Sometimes a positive tone is difficult to achieve. Role-playing is helpful in becoming more adept and confident in using these communication skills.

Here is one example of replacing an aggressive response with an assertive one. Instead of saying: "I hate that you are always playing games when I come home from work," you could state, "I really love it when I come home and you talk to me about your day." The second statement indicates what *you* want *briefly* and *clearly*. It uses a *positive tone*. It even mentions *your feelings*.

Another example is of a father who yells at his son about his gaming. A typical statement he makes might be, "I can't believe you stayed up until all hours last night playing those games again. Don't you have anything better to do? You're going to fail out of school if you keep that up." Instead, he could state, "I can see that you didn't get a lot of sleep last night. I know I usually accuse you of gaming when you are tired. I also know this upsets you, so I will try to give you a chance to explain before I jump to conclusions." This statement offers an *understanding statement* and *accepts partial responsibility* for the problem.

Consider another father who tells his child, "I hate that you waste away every afternoon playing those games." He could alter his comments to, "I wish I could come home from work earlier so that you would not have to be alone so much. I can't get home before 6, but let's talk about some ways we can spend more time together doing things we both enjoy when I am home." This statement is *brief, clear, accepts partial responsibility,* and *labels the parent's feelings*.

Now, think about examples of things you have said to your child about his or her gaming. List them in Worksheet 7.3. Think of some alternative ways of addressing issues that arise. Which of the communication aids listed above do the new responses include?

Imagine how your child would respond to the alternate statement rather than your usual approach. Envision how you will feel after using a more positive tone. Make a commitment to try one of the positive responses the next time a troubling issue arises. Consider likely scenarios over the next few days or weeks, and brainstorm new responses using these communication aids.

Think about these communication skills and aids as you read Chapters 8 to 10. Over the next several weeks, record on Worksheet 7.4 situations that arise that had potential for conflict. Indicate how you responded to them passively, aggressively, or assertively. If any denial, enabling, or bailout behaviors occur, also try to label them as such. How did your child respond to your reactions? How did you feel after each encounter? If you did not feel good about the way the interaction went, how could you have responded differently or more assertively?

Considering your own communication styles is not easy. However, the more often you do it, the easier it will become. If it is

Worksheet 7.3
Communication aids for new response to video game playing

<u>Communication Aids:</u>

1. Be brief, specific and clear.
2. Be positive.
3. Use "I" instead of "you" statements.
4. Give a rationale.
5. Provide an understanding statement of another perspective.
6. Balance negative with positive.
7. Offer to help when possible.
8. Speak firmly.
9. Respond promptly.
10. Deliver a consistent message.

Instead of:	I could say (alternate response):	Communication aid(s):	Possible reactions:
Example: Yelling at him that he isn't coming to dinner.	"I'm sorry I made dinner when you weren't hungry. Next time, I'll ask you if you want to eat with us, and if not, just let me know so I don't make more than needed."	Brief, specific and clear; Uses "I" statements; Gives rationale; Provides understanding of another perspective; Offers to help; Firm; Prompt.	He may say he never wants to eat dinner with our family again. He may say he wants dinner, and then still not eat if he's in the middle of a game. I could then throw his away, and at least I'm not enabling playing.

Instead of:	I could say (alternate response):	Communication aid(s):	Possible reactions:

Worksheet 7.4
Tracking responses and communication styles

Situation with potential for conflict	Your response	Was it passive, aggressive, or assertive? Did it involve denial, enabling, or bailouts?	How did it make you feel?	How did your child react?	If it did not go well, how could you have responded differently?
Example: I got home late; he hadn't made dinner as promised.	I blew up and yelled.	Aggressive.	Horrible.	He slammed the door.	I could have said, "I remember you told me at 4:00 that you were going to make dinner tonight. You must have got caught up in a game and forgot how late it is. Please start dinner now. I'm starving. You must be too."
Example: My child overslept probably because of a late night playing games.	I woke him up so he wouldn't be late for school.	Passive (and enabling).	At least he didn't get a 0 on his test today.	He was groggy and seemed annoyed that I woke him up.	I could wake him up, but I also remind him of our "Getting up and game playing contract." I could say, "I'm waking you up so you don't miss school, but this goes against what we agreed. You need to use your alarm clock. I don't know if you were playing games late last night or not, but our agreement was that if you didn't get up on your own, I would take the Nintendo away for 1 month. You can have it back in a month if you wake up on your own for the next month."

easiest for you to think back each night before you go to bed about these issues, then use that time to reflect. If first thing in the morning works better, make a habit of taking a few moments early in the day to think about the prior day. Once you can start to pinpoint assertive responses, you will feel better about them, and they will begin to feel more natural. Consider any situation in which you responded assertively, whether it was with a coworker, a friend or acquaintance, your partner or another family member, or your child. Give yourself a pat on the back for each assertive response. Even if you go a day or a few days without an assertive response, know that you are making positive strides by reflecting on your communication patterns.

Remember that communication skills take time to develop and learn, and no one behaves assertively in all situations. There may be times when you responded assertively, but the situation still did not go well or as planned. There may be other times that you fell back into the trap of passive or enabling responses, and sometimes even aggressive ones. The important thing is that you recognize them as such. The more you react in an assertive manner, the more likely your relationship with your child will improve. As your relationship progresses in a more positive direction, there is a greater likelihood that gaming will decrease, along with the problems that come with it.

8

Step 1—Record: How to monitor and set limits on gaming

Pete came to realize that his aggressive personality style was not helping the situation with his son. Amy admitted that she had been too passive about their son's gaming and rarely, if ever, brought it up with him. Amy also didn't believe Sam was gaming as much as Pete said he was; she thought it was considerably less time, as he often was using the computer for things other than just gaming. They both agreed to use the communication tips in Chapter 7 in their interactions with each other, as well as with their son, as they moved forward in addressing the gaming issue. Pete, however, felt that his son needed to stop gaming completely, while Amy thought it was fine for him to continue playing as long as it wasn't interfering with his schoolwork and other responsibilities. She knew all his friends played, and taking gaming away completely would make him feel different and isolated; she was worried that a complete removal of gaming would make her son think he was being punished. Their first compromise was to agree to determine how much Sam was actually gaming prior to deciding upon appropriate limits.

Improving communication styles (Chapter 7) is the basis for beginning to help your child overcome his or her problems with gaming. This chapter and the next two outline specific steps that you can take to help your child overcome gaming problems. These three steps are:

(1) Record
(2) Replace
(3) Reward

While reading these chapters, consider what you learned in the last chapter. Try to use assertive response styles whenever possible in implementing these steps.

Do not expect the techniques to stop all gaming immediately or entirely. Just as it took time for problems to develop, it will also take time for them to resolve. If your child has severe problems with gaming, these steps alone may not be sufficient, but they should still be helpful. If your child has other behavioral or mental health disorders in addition to Internet gaming disorder, then you will likely need professional support as Chapter 6 describes. You can still apply many of these suggestions, but your child may need specific treatment for depression, anxiety, or ADHD. Depending on the severity of problems, the initial intervention may need to be intensive, perhaps requiring inpatient care if your child is suicidal or in imminent danger.

However, most kids with gaming problems do not have these extreme difficulties. Many children play games regularly, and although some problems may arise, concerns are usually relatively modest. The three steps mentioned above should be helpful in reducing difficulties in many children who are experiencing some problems with gaming, especially if you practice them diligently and give them time to work.

You can also apply the techniques preventively. If you are concerned that your teenage, preteen, or younger child may develop problems with video games, it is never too early to take precautions. In fact, instituting rules for gaming and technology use more broadly, as well as developing good communication skills around these issues, is the best prevention.

You need not undertake all three steps, or do them in the suggested order. You may find that carrying out just a couple of them is sufficient. You may also prefer to implement them in a different order. For example, you may introduce the first step (Record) and third step (Reward, Chapter 10) more or less simultaneously. After seeing some progress, you may then integrate the second step

(Chapter 9, Replace). Alternatively, you may find that implementing Steps 1 and 2 (Record and Replace) is sufficient, and you may decide not to institute Step 3 (Reward).

At the extreme end of the spectrum, you may feel that you already know how much your child is playing—he is playing all the time! Rather than spending 2 weeks better understanding his pattern of play by recording, you may decide to move immediately to a complete ban on video gaming (see Chapter 11, on extreme cases). Even in this case, you will benefit by reviewing and instituting the suggestions contained in this chapter and in Chapters 9 and 10, because replacing and rewarding nongaming behaviors will help your child adjust to a new life without gaming.

How you choose to employ the recommendations is up to you. You know your child better than anyone else. Each step takes time, and some take practice. The more thoroughly and consistently you integrate these suggestions, the greater the likelihood that you will begin to see changes in your child's gaming behaviors.

Educating yourself about your child's gaming

This section details things that you, as a parent, can do to better realize the extent of your child's gaming frequencies and durations. Parental monitoring can impact children's behavior in a positive manner.[1] Parental monitoring of children's media usage, including gaming, can improve academic performance, social functioning, and sleep time.[2]

Once you have a better understanding of how much and how often your child is gaming, you can encourage him or her to be a partner in the process of raising awareness of and recording gaming times. This chapter describes this process. It also outlines how explicitly you can set reasonable rules and guidelines regarding gaming, depending on how old your child is. The goals and consequences may vary based on the age of your child, but the procedures have similar components.

Record gaming in a log

The first step, and the focus of this chapter, relates to **Recording gaming activities.** You want to raise your own awareness of the actual level of playing. You know your child is gaming a lot, but it may be hard to pin down an actual time frame by day or by week. By keeping a log, you will not only better understand how much your child is gaming, but you will also begin to identify *patterns* in the behavior. Once you uncover some regularity to the gaming, you will be in a better position to address it assertively with your child and thereby modify it.

Although you cannot be with your child all day every day, you can still take several measures to ensure that you have a fairly good understanding of how much time he or she is gaming while you are around. The amount of gaming that takes place when you are at home and aware of it may be only a fraction of the time your child is actually playing. Therefore, the more you are able to track it directly, the closer your estimates will be to reality.

Ideally, you want to keep a log of gaming activities. The log should record the amount of time spent gaming each day. Recording information for just a few weekdays may not be representative of gaming that occurs on the weekends or vice versa. The week or day that you initiated the recording process may be unusual in some regard, especially if it occurs in direct relation to an argument you had with your child when she was playing more, such as during a school vacation. You should record the amount of gaming time for at least 2 weeks, and ideally 2 "typical" weeks, until you start to see some consistency in the times.

Worksheet 8.1 provides a recording log. It breaks each day into subsections or times representing earlier and later mornings, afternoons, and evenings. The expectation is not that you will be able to check on your child at all these specified times throughout every day. The worksheet asks you to list the times you *were* able to check and indicate "Yes" or "No" in terms of whether or not he was gaming each time you did check. If you miss checking for an entire period of the day, that is fine. For example, you may be unable to ascertain the time spent gaming between 7 a.m. and 3:30 p.m. on most days if you work during those hours. Just leave that area blank on the days you could not check at those times. If you check more than once in a time frame, indicate both times you checked and whether or not your child was gaming. If you check at a particular time and he is *not* gaming, it is just as important to note the time and a "No" response as it is to list "Yes" when gaming is occurring. By checking as much as feasible throughout the day, you will start to see patterns in gaming behaviors. You will also be able to discern patterns related to when gaming *does not* occur.

Let's consider the case of Sam. Sam's mother began recording when her son was gaming, as shown in Worksheet 8.2. Each time Sam's mother checked on him she wrote down the time in the appropriate section of the row for that day and "Yes" or "No" depending on whether or not he was gaming next to each time. The first morning she checked on him, on Tuesday, was a holiday, as indicated in the Notes section, so they were both at home. Sam was playing at 10 a.m., and had stopped by 11 a.m. He was not gaming when she checked in on him again at noon and 3 p.m. nor was he playing right before dinner at 6 p.m. However, when she went to his room to say goodnight to him at 11 p.m., he was gaming. In the final column, Sam's mother estimated that he played at least 3 hours that day.

Sam's mother continued recording her son's gaming in this same manner for the next 6 days. His dad also monitored gaming on the evening he was with him that week. Sam did not seem to play first thing in the morning. On the four early mornings when his mother checked, he was never gaming.

According to the weekly log, however, Sam did start gaming before noon on 2 days of the week. On school days, he was often

Worksheet 8.1
Weekly recording logs

Week of ____ / ____ / ____ to ____ / ____ / ____

Time of day

Day	6 am – 9 am	10 am – 12 pm	12 pm – 2 pm	2 pm – 4 pm	4 pm – 6 pm	6 pm – 8 pm	8 pm – 10 pm	10 pm – 12 am	12 am – 6 am	Total hrs

Notes:

Week of ____ / ____ / ____ to ____ / ____ / ____

Time of day

Day	6 am – 9 am	10 am – 12 pm	12 pm – 2 pm	2 pm – 4 pm	4 pm – 6 pm	6 pm – 8 pm	8 pm – 10 pm	10 pm – 12 am	12 am – 6 am	Total hrs

Notes:

Worksheet 8.2
Sample completed weekly recording log

Time of day

Day	6 am – 9 am	10 am – 12 pm	12 pm – 2 pm	2 pm – 4 pm	4 pm – 6 pm	6 pm – 8 pm	8 pm – 10 pm	10 pm – 12 am	12 am – 6 am	Total hrs
Tues		10 Yes, 11 No	12 No	3 No		6 No		11 Yes		3+ hrs
Wed	7:30 No			3:30 No	4:30 Yes	6 No	9 Yes		1 Yes	4+ hrs
Thur	7 No			3:30 No		6 No	9 Yes	10:30 Yes		2+ hrs
Fri					4 Yes	7 No	10 No	11 No		1 hr
Sat	9 No	11 Yes	1 Yes	3 No	4:30 Yes	6 No, 7 Yes	9 Yes	10:30 Yes		7+ hrs
Sun	9 No	11 No	12 No 1 Yes	3 No			8 Yes			3+ hrs
Mon				3:30 No	5 Yes	6 Yes	8 Yes			3+ hrs

Notes: Tuesday was a school holiday, and we had a doctor's appointment that afternoon.
Wednesday evening I took him to his dad's house at 6, and his dad found him gaming at 9 p.m. and midnight.
Friday night he went out with friends.
I don't know what time he stops playing late at night.

gaming by about 4 p.m., but not immediately when his mother got home from work at about 3:30, as these checks are generally negative. The evenings appear to be the most likely time for Sam to game. On five of the six nights his parents checked, he was playing by 8 or 10 p.m., often persisting throughout the evening. The only night that Sam was not gaming was Friday, because he went out with friends.

You can indicate issues or events that interrupted or prevented typical gaming behaviors at the bottom of the worksheets. These notes will help you uncover unique circumstances that may relate to gaming or not gaming. In later chapters you can come back to your notes in these logs to generate ideas about activities that may be substituted for, and prevent, gaming in the future.

You may be tempted to simply ask your child about how much he is gaming. However, many kids do not recognize how much they are actually gaming, or they may cover up their behaviors. Asking directly about gaming may not yield accurate reporting. In fact, lying to others to hide the extent of gaming is a symptom of Internet gaming disorder (see Chapters 3 and 6).

You may feel uncomfortable about tracking your child's behavior. You may feel that it is like spying or violating his or her privacy. The goal of the log, however, is to ascertain the amount of time your child is gaming with some degree of accuracy. Table 8.1 can help you to consider both the pros and cons of tracking your child's gaming. Feel free to add to the list provided in the table.

There are valid reasons to—and not to—track your child's behavior, and this process can be a valuable tool if it is used in the right way. Importantly, by having a good "baseline" indicator of your child's behavior, you will be assured about whether gaming is increasing or decreasing as you institute other changes.

How to accurately measure gaming

There are three ways you can determine the frequency (although not necessarily the exact durations) of gaming. You can observe it in

TABLE 8.1 Pros and cons of tracking your child's gaming

Cons	Pros
It seems like spying on my child.	I want to be able to trust my child, and this method allows me to learn the true extent of gaming.
I don't have the time (or ability) to track my child. I am rarely home when he is, and I am sleeping when he is most often gaming.	Tracking may be the first step in better understanding what is going on. I can make an effort to check at least three times a day when I am home at the same time as my child.
I might get into arguments with my child about how much he games.	I will not use this information to confront my child, only to help him. I can determine patterns in my child's behavior, which I can use to help break those patterns. My goal by tracking is to help my child.
I'm afraid that my child may be gaming even more than I thought.	If my child is gaming even more than I thought, I will know there will need to be changes. I can use this information to determine if the problems are getting worse or better over time.
Your examples:	

its natural environment, as Sam's mother did in the example above, attempting to check on her son's game-playing behaviors as they were occurring. Two other approaches are (1) restructuring the environment to better witness it and (2) checking browser histories. The next two sections describe these latter two tracking methods.

Restructuring the environment

You can best know if your child is gaming if you can see what she or he is doing. Sam's mother, in our example above, was only able to see whether or not Sam was gaming by going into his room, because he most often used the laptop there. He played games nearly exclusively in his bedroom. Clearly, she probably missed a lot of times he was playing simply because she could not see what he was doing.

You can consider restructuring your home environment to increase your ability to record gaming behaviors. Rearranging your house can raise your awareness of the location of all devices on which your child plays. If you know where electronic devices are, including all mobile devices, you will become more cognizant of when they are being used, and the purposes for which your child is using them. Not only will reorganizing electronics assist you in tracking behaviors, it will reduce gaming naturally by decreasing unmonitored accessibility to these devices. When no one can see what kids are doing, social controls on excessive behaviors are lacking. To the extent that you can make gaming a more open activity in your home, social controls will begin to modulate it.

To facilitate awareness and use of gaming devices, you can create a central storage area for electronics. If you keep laptops, iPads, and smartphones on a desk in the kitchen or table in the living room, as opposed to letting them stay in your child's bedroom, you can monitor their whereabouts and their use more directly. You may consider purchasing a table or desk for the entryway, kitchen, or living room, along with a new docking or charging station to facilitate this change. There are paper towel holders with plug-in capacity so that devices can be charged on the kitchen counter. As family members arrive home after school or work, they can put their phones into a basket or recharger. By having a "home" for this equipment in a common area, you will know where each device is. You can monitor use of devices when you know where they are. Whenever they are not in use, no one is gaming on them.

You can discuss upfront with your child why you are making these changes. Using assertive communication skills, you can directly state you are worried about how much your child is gaming. By storing all devices in one spot, you can tell your child that he can now prove to you all the times he is not playing on them. You will also vow to no longer accuse him of playing when he is not! You all will be better off knowing exactly when gaming is not occurring.

Another, less direct but still realistic, rationale for instituting a home storage base for electronic equipment relates to minimization of loss. Power cords and devices themselves are often misplaced. By storing them centrally, this concern can be reduced. Another possible rationale relates to clutter. A makeover of your home environment, for aesthetics or better organization, may be the first step toward knowing where, when, and how often your child is gaming.

In terms of other organizational issues, a desktop computer could be relocated from a bedroom to another room or area of the house that is common, but quiet, for school or work purposes. With children and teenagers and only when necessary, you can grant permission to take laptops into other private or quiet areas, but only with doors open. You can then make random but frequent check-ins. Some parents may find checking up on their child to be invasive, and clearly all kids will—especially if it is framed in that manner. However, if you felt your child were in imminent danger with regard to some other behavior, you would likely have no problem checking in on him, even if he didn't like your oversight. If you feel your child's gaming is harming him, you should feel justified in changing your behaviors for the good of your child. If this means checking in frequently on how he is using his computer or insisting on an open-door policy during all electronics usage, then that is an appropriate step. Again, assertive communication skills can be helpful in this regard.

When your child is using computers or smartphones for non-school-related purposes such as social media, surfing the Internet, and gaming, you can (and should!) restrict use to common areas for closer observation. Again, this may be a new household rule that is met with some resistance, but it is not unreasonable. There is no reason kids *must* text in their rooms. They can just as easily text their friends in the living room, but doing so will likely require diligence and frequent corrections on your part, at least initially. To the extent possible, limit access to all electronic devices—except for agreed-upon and necessary activities—when you cannot directly observe them. The latter parts of this chapter provide tips on how to institute healthy rules for gaming.

Restricting electronics use to nonprivate areas in the home is the best prevention of overuse and misuse. Having a video game system in a bedroom is associated with greater gaming.[3] In addition, adolescents with video games in their bedrooms are more likely to play violent or mature-rated games than those without game access in their rooms.[4] Although teenagers love privacy, unmonitored use of electronics facilitates their inappropriate use.

Returning to the case of Sam, his mother was attempting to record when he was and was not gaming. To get a better sense of how often Sam was actually gaming so that ultimately she could help him decrease this time, Sam's mother decided to reorganize the house. She told Sam that his room was too small to contain all his belongings, including his desk, dresser, and other things. She informed him that she thought he would be more comfortable and productive with his schoolwork if he used the family room as his new study. Together, they moved his desk to the family room, which did not have a door. They relocated his computer to the family room as well.

Sam was initially thrilled at the thought of getting an extra room to himself, when it was presented in this way. Sam's mom reminded him that having the family room as his "office," however, was a privilege. He needed to focus on his studies there. He was to keep the laptop there and do his homework on it. To maintain use of the family room, he had to promise to not turn the television on while doing homework. His mother told him that she thought he would be less likely to fall asleep while using the computer there compared to in his bedroom, and this would help with his studies as well.

By moving Sam's desk and computer into a more public area of the home, Sam's mother could much more easily see what he was doing and when. His bedroom became a room dedicated for sleeping, and not for activities such as gaming.

Even if you cannot dedicate a room in your home to one child, you can institute other measures to better monitor electronics usage. These will include promoting the return of each device to its storage location after use and eliminating or minimizing access to gaming devices in bedrooms. This process clearly will entail frequent corrections, from you as well as other family members. In two-parent families, it is particularly important that both parents be on board and enforce the same rules in the same manner. Even in a shared custody situation, it is ideal that both parents monitor the child while she or he is with each one. Gaming may vary drastically in different households and environments.

In this case, Sam's father also agreed to keep a log of gaming times whenever Sam was over at his place. He may have noticed that Sam also spent a lot of time in his bedroom there, presumably gaming. Sam's dad likewise may have instituted new household rules that the laptop remain in common rooms so that he could more directly observe its use. Pete may say to his son,

> *"Sam, just like at your mom's house, we are no longer going to use computers or any electronics in the bedrooms. I'm going to follow this*

rule too, and if I need to answer a text or email, I will do it in the kitchen or living room. If you have homework to do, you can do it here, at my desk. We aren't together all that much, and when you are here, I want us to really be together."

Although change, including keeping better tabs on what your child is doing and restructuring your home to do so, can be hard, remember that your current home setup *facilitated* the gaming behaviors that are now causing concerns. Altering the environment is one of the best ways, and ultimately perhaps the simplest, to change these behaviors.

Reviewing browser histories

If you are unable to know where each device is or how it is being used during most days, a last-resort strategy involves checking the browser history. If online games are accessed, these activities are recorded by a computer's browser. Box 8.1 describes how you can access browser histories on PCs and Apple devices.

This search should inform you whether or not the device was used to game, and provide information about the specific games played and when. If laptops, tablets, and smartphones are stored in a centralized area, checking histories will be easier. However, this is not a foolproof method to ascertain gaming, as browser histories can be deleted. Your child may be deleting browser histories, especially if he suspects you are checking them.

You should be aware that you may uncover activities that may alarm you by checking browser histories. Your child may be viewing pornography or other sites, and these, too, will be detailed on the histories. Before you check histories, you may want to consider the pros and cons of looking and what you hope to gain by doing so. If you are truly concerned about gaming and this is one of the only methods by which you can ascertain it, you may believe the ends justify the means. On the other hand, you may

BOX 8.1. Accessing browser histories

Browser histories are stored on computers and other electronic devices (e.g., iPads) and indicate recent sites visited, usually for the past 90 days. They show all the sites visited, including by dates.

To access the browser history on personal computers (PCs), open Internet Explorer and view the "history" button, which will be located near (often to the right and immediately below) the area in which you type in search words. If you click on "manage history," you will get a list of recently viewed webpages. You can click "View," "Explorer Bar," then "History," or use a shortcut—Ctrl+Shift+H. You can view the history by date, site, order visited, or most often visited. With the Firefox browser, click on the "History" tab, and then on "Show All History," or use the same shortcut: Ctrl+Shift+H. Again, you can organize this list by selecting column headers like "last visited," "date added," etc. to see which sites were accessed when. The Google browsing history tool also lets you sort history according to content such as images, products, maps, blogs, etc. If you click on "trends," you can see the most searched-for items and a breakdown of when searches happened, down to the hour of each day.

You can similarly check browsing histories for Apple or Mac computers as well. For example, if your computer uses Safari, open it, hit "Alternate" and click on "History" in the menu bar, then "Show All." You can check online resources for accessing the browser histories of other operating systems if these tips don't work.

feel that checking devices directly is an invasion of privacy, especially for adult children. Other methods, such as the monitoring outlined earlier, may be sufficient to gain the information you need to help to reduce gaming.

If you do decide to check browser histories, you may not be able to do so if the device is password protected and you do not know the password or username. Creation of a master list of the usernames and passwords of all devices can help prevent problems, and possibly even deter inappropriate use of devices. Family members can still have private passwords to email, social media, and other personal accounts if this is appropriate given the age of your child. Parents who have the ability to monitor their children's electronic devices have better knowledge of and control over their children's electronics usage than those who do not.

Establishing your authority to access devices is easiest when you first buy the device. Purchase can be contingent upon all family members being able to use them, even if they are designated for a specific person. If one person is primarily using a computer, tablet, or smartphone, other family members should be able to use it if they need to. A single family password for all electronic devices can work well in some circumstances. If different devices require different passwords, then others should know them. Having such a discussion about the need to keep records of all passwords, and regularly checking them to ensure they work and are not changed over time, will ensure their functionality. These practices will also allow parents access to their children's electronics to know *how* they are using them. The simple knowledge that a parent has control over a device may be enough to deter some children from using it in a manner they would not want their parent to uncover.

Even if you have never examined your child's electronics previously, it is not too late to start. You can discuss the need to record all usernames and passwords proactively, or when you make your next electronics purchase for your home, explain how all electronics will be used moving forward.

Let's consider the case of an older teen or young adult, Tim, and assume that his mother did not know his username or password. She could not get onto his laptop to check his browser histories. After recording his gaming behavior for a week, Tim's mother realized she was lacking a good understanding of what he was doing on his laptop. One night at dinner, when nothing controversial had happened that day, Tim's mom said,

> *"Tim, I may have to use your computer at times, and I also want to be able to be sure you are only using electronic devices for things you should be using them for. I should have done this earlier when I first got them for you. I want you to give me the usernames and passwords for your computer, iPad, and iPhone. I don't need your passwords to specific sites, like your Facebook account, but I need to be able to get onto all your devices. I'd like you to write them down here. I'll keep the list here in this drawer, and you'll just need to let me know if you change any. I'll be checking them every once in a while, and if you aren't using them for anything that you shouldn't be there won't be any problems."*

In this manner, Tim's mother was not demanding or accusatory. She provided a rational reason why usernames and passwords should be recorded. Because Tim was an older teenager, his mother did not ask him to include his Facebook, email, or other private account information, just methods for accessing devices. For younger teens or children, parents may feel justified in having all their children's passwords. With new information about how to access computers, Tim's mother could now much more closely monitor how frequently he was gaming.

After completing the gaming recording sheet for a few weeks via direct observation with or without also monitoring browser histories, you will have a much more realistic idea about the extent to which your child is gaming. By understanding the patterns of play, you will be better equipped to reduce it. Look for times during the day that gaming is most likely to begin, and times it is most likely to end. See if there is any regularity to the episodes. School or work days may differ from weekends, or days with few structured activities. Once you see some general patterns, you then will be in a better position to talk with your child about your observations and help him understand the extent of the gaming and your concerns.

Most parents are able to monitor their child's gaming at least some of the time for several weeks. If you feel unable or unwilling to do so, please see Box 8.2.

BOX 8.2. What if you just can't bear to monitor your child's gaming?

Research shows, and experiences confirm, that one of the best ways to change a behavior is to monitor it frequently. However, some parents may feel that regular monitoring is just something they cannot do. Reasons can range from not wanting to, feeling too busy, or perceiving monitoring to be unhelpful or not useful. Regardless of your rationales, you can still apply other steps in this book even if you don't want to (or can't, if your child doesn't live with you) monitor your child's gaming behaviors. The Replace and Reward steps, covered in Chapters 9 and 10, can be applied even without monitoring. However, you should know that they work better when combined with regular monitoring.

If you are on the fence about monitoring, consider trying it for a limited time period. In other words, commit to monitoring for just 1 or 2 weeks. Many people find that once they get into the habit, monitoring becomes easier with time. Also, monitoring just once a day (e.g., before bed or first thing in the morning) is easier than trying to remember to do it throughout the day. If you can monitor your child's behavior at least once a day for at least 1 week, that will put you in a better position to understand the baseline levels of your child's gaming. You will have this week (or 2) to reflect back on as you begin instituting other changes.

If you truly do not want to monitor your child's gaming, consider asking another adult in the household to do so. If that is impossible, you may be inclined to rely on your child's own monitoring. Although the next section outlines actions your child can take and encourages children to do their own monitoring of their gaming, remember that any monitoring completed by your child may be subject to error. Kids can and do try to cover up their gaming from their parents. Monitoring of gaming by your child may be preferable to no monitoring, but only if you attempt to validate your child's reports. Use this approach cautiously, as you do not want to be basing rewards (Chapter 10) and other decisions on incorrect information.

How can my child participate?

The preceding sections describe actions that you can take to better understand and help your child. If you have monitored gaming for several weeks, you should begin to uncover patterns of play. This next section will help you to encourage your child to record his own gaming so he can be an active participant in the process. If he begins to recognize the extent of gaming, he may be likely to acknowledge problems with it. This section is most relevant to older adolescents and adult children. If you have a younger child, you may move directly to the last section in this chapter. It describes methods for setting and presenting limits.

Recognize the extent of playing

Kids who play video games for more than 5 days a week or more than 20 hours per week are more likely to develop Internet gaming disorder than those who play less frequently and for shorter durations.[5] If gaming has not yet resulted in significant problems, your child may be unwilling to accept the possibility that gaming holds the potential to cause difficulties. Even in these cases, a discussion can be useful about the actual amount of playing.

If you have monitored gaming for several weeks, you can provide reasonable estimates to your child using a nonjudgmental tone. The discussion may go something like this:

"I've been noticing that you are playing games every day or nearly every day. My guess is that you are probably playing for 20 hours a week. Would you agree with those estimates?"

If your opening line is matter-of-fact and nonthreatening, your child may be more willing to participate in an honest dialogue.

If your child admits to gaming as much or more than what you mentioned, you are in a good position to begin asking about problems or difficulties that may have arisen from it. Now may also be a good time to ask about the symptoms of Internet gaming disorder, outlined in Chapter 3. At this time, you may feel comfortable telling your child that you found a questionnaire (Worksheet 6.1) that relates to problems that sometimes arise from gaming. You may ask your child to make his own appraisal of his gaming.

Tim's mother, for example, recorded his gaming as often as she could for 2 weeks. After checking browser histories, she realized that the days and times he played were even higher than she originally estimated. In her first week of monitoring, she thought he was playing about 26 hours per week. In the second week, when she checked more consistently, her estimate increased to over 30 hours.

She initiated a discussion with her son the next weekend. At breakfast, she said to him,

> *"Tim, it seems like you may be gaming more often than you used to. I know you like playing these games. This past week, it seems to me like you've been gaming about 3 to 4 hours a day on average. Would you say that is a fair estimate?"*

Tim may initially deny that he is gaming anywhere near that much. Although his mother stated the estimate in a nonjudgmental manner, Tim may get defensive. He may argue that he is only gaming to relax, that he only games after he finishes his schoolwork, that he isn't gaming any more than anyone else he knows, or that it is none of her business what he does in his free time. Rather than arguing with him about any of these specific issues, Tim's mother will do best by not focusing on his rationalizations for gaming, but instead by encouraging him to estimate how much he thinks he is gaming. She might say,

> *"I'm not criticizing you—really I'm not. I just want to get a sense from you how much you think you are gaming."*

If Tim responds that he is gaming daily or nearly every day, but he substantially decreases the time estimates to far less than 3 to 4 hours a day, his mother may ask him to keep a log, just for himself, about how much he is gaming. She may introduce the exercise like this:

> *"Only you can know how much you are gaming and whether or not you really want to be playing as much as you are. How about keeping track of when you game and how long, just for a week? Try this for your own sake. Each time after you play, write down the time you stopped and estimate the time you started. If you do this for 1 week, you'll know how*

much you're actually gaming. You'll also know if it is more than you want to be. Are there other things you'd rather be doing with some of this time? As you see how much you're really gaming, you may begin to think about it differently."

If Tim refuses to record his gaming for an entire week, his mother may suggest he try it just for a couple of days. Over the course of the next few days or week, Tim's mother may remind him to record how much he is gaming. On days she knows he is gaming a lot, she might ask him the next day,

"Did you remember to keep track of how much you played yesterday? Let's mark it down here, because if you wait you'll forget what happened each day."

If your child will not consider tracking his gaming at all, then offer to do it with him. Even if you monitor with your child, you can still maintain your own independent record log as described earlier. Having two sources of information is always better than one. At the end of the week, Tim's mother might say,

"I know I've been asking you record each day how much you've been gaming, and I know it's been annoying to you. But did you learn anything about how much you are actually gaming? Is it an amount you are comfortable with?"

If at any point Tim expresses regret, concern, or surprise about how much he is gaming, his mother should commend his self-discovery. The tone should never be, "I told you so!" Instead, statements should reflect caring and concern, along with a willingness to help. Tim may admit at the end of the week, *"Okay, you were right. I did play about 20 hours last week."*

To such a statement, his mother may reply,

> *"I am glad we agree about the time. I thought it seemed about that much. Do you think this is a good amount? Or, are there other things you'd rather be doing with some of that time?"*

There are two ways Tim could respond to such a question. He could affirm that there is nothing wrong with how much he is gaming. He could also state it seems more than he thought, thereby acknowledging at least some degree of excess in his behavior. Even in the former case, his mother could say,

> *"I found a survey about gaming and how it can affect people. I know you don't think you are gaming too much, but why don't you take a look at it and see if any of these issues apply. If not, that is great. But, if you do feel like the answer to any of these questions might be 'yes,' you may want to think about changing how much or how often you are gaming. Only you will know the answers to these questions. These are some of the things that can happen when people are gaming too much."*

Tie in extent of gaming with problems

Tim's mother may give him Worksheet 6.1 to complete on his own. If he admits to any adverse effects of gaming, his mother can use his realizations to come to an agreement about how much time is appropriate. Using the items he circles "yes" on, she can discuss preferred levels of gaming that may help alleviate issues that he identifies.

On Worksheet 6.1, let's assume that Tim admitted to thinking about gaming even while he was not gaming (1a), planning when he could next play (1b), and not getting enough sleep because of gaming (6a). These responses would give him a score of 2 (1 point for criterion 1 and 1 point for criterion 6), and put him in an "at risk" category. His mother might then use that information to encourage him to try putting some limits on how much he is gaming so that these issues do not become more pronounced and so that additional problems do not emerge. She may introduce the conversation in this manner:

> "I, too, can see that you sometimes seem to be preoccupied with gaming, and you are gaming until very late at night. I'm not surprised you feel like you are losing out on sleep. Let's see what we can do to try to make sure your gaming doesn't lead to other problems, like poor grades at school or missing out on other things you like to do with friends. What do you think about setting a time limit at night when you think you should stop playing, like 10 p.m.? How about also playing only a certain number of nights each week, and taking a day off from playing at least a couple nights a week?"

If you have an older child in a similar situation, think about how he may respond to this question. If you think his reaction would be positive, try a similar conversation. If you don't think it would lead to a good result, try another approach using other assertive communication skills.

Setting limits on gaming

In terms of safe limits to gaming, your ideas may not match your child's, but if your child agrees that a level lower than he is currently playing is preferred, this is definitely a move in the right direction. You may suggest no playing or playing only once a week for an hour, but that expectation may not be consistent with his. If your child is an adult, it is best to let him suggest a goal. A self-selected goal is more likely to be reached than one imposed by others. Maintaining the current level of gaming can even be reasonable in some cases;

if gaming does not increase, it is unlikely to lead to a worsening of symptoms or problems.

If you are concerned about a younger child, you can (and should!) more directly regulate gaming. You may not be able to prevent it completely, such as when your child is at friends' houses. Nevertheless, if you are able to successfully limit gaming in your own home, this is a positive initial step toward preventing excessive playing.

Determining and enforcing limits for kids

For children and younger adolescents, and even for older adolescents under the age of 18 years, you as a parent should have the bulk of the say in determining appropriate limits to gaming. Having clear and consistent guidelines related to gaming prevents excessive playing. One study[6] found that parents who reported having *specific* and *well-defined* limits on gaming noted their children were less likely to play excessively than children of parents without clear limits. However, two-thirds of US children and adolescents indicate that their parents have "no rules" related to time spent on media use.[7] Be sure you are no longer part of that majority!

There is no single well-defined limit on gaming time that prevents harm. The rules you select for your child will vary depending on the age of your child, the severity of problems she or he is experiencing, and your preferences and family lifestyle. Some tips for developing gaming rules are shown in Box 8.3.

The tips in Box 8.3 allow for some gaming, but they require that you accurately and consistently record gaming frequencies and durations. If you decide that your child should play *no* video games at all, temporarily or permanently, Chapter 11 describes how to go about making this process happen. Even if you elect for a complete ban on gaming, please review Chapters 9 and 10 for additional suggestions that can help your child develop a new lifestyle without gaming.

> **BOX 8.3.** Tips for developing game-playing rules
>
> 1. Game playing should occur only after responsibilities are completed.
> 2. Specify the duration of maximum play for each day.
> 3. Include a time frame to reassess goals.
> 4. Provide realistic consequences for nonadherence.
> 5. Know and approve of the games your child is playing.
> 6. Ensure consistent monitoring and enforcement of the contract.

If you do feel comfortable with limited gaming for your child, consider the guidelines in Box 8.3, further described here:

1. Remember that gaming should occur only *after* your child completes his or her other responsibilities for the day, including homework and household chores. Be sure to check the quality and completeness of homework and housework prior to allowing your child to begin playing. Relatedly, playing video games should be a privilege that is earned. Gaming is not an inalienable right!

2. Put clear limits on your child's gaming. The Council on Communications and Media[8] suggests time allotted should be under 30 to 60 minutes per day on school days and 2 hours or less on non-school days. The American Academy of Pediatrics[9] recommends even lower limits of under 1 hour of total screen time per day for children under 6 years old, and they encourage parents to determine the appropriate amount of time for gaming and other electronic media use for children over the age of 6. They provide an online planner to assist parents in deciding on screen time: https://www.healthychildren.org/English/media/Pages/default.aspx. Regardless of what limits you think are appropriate, **some days each week should involve no gaming**. It is crucial to ensure that your child develops, maintains, and enjoys other, non-screen-time activities. This is an issue that Chapter 9 describes in greater depth.

No matter what limits you select, be clear about the times and the days, especially if you permit different amounts of time depending on the day such as school days versus weekends. You should also consider school holiday and vacation days explicitly in your plan. For example, if you think 2 hours of game playing is reasonable on non-school days, does this apply to Fridays, school holidays, and every day during spring and summer breaks? Or, does the 2-hour rule only relate to Saturdays and Sundays?

Timers on cell phones, computers, or other devices can be useful in monitoring gaming and enforcing gaming rules. Preset timers can signal the end or near end of a gaming episode, and timers may also help some children prepare for a transition to another activity. Because games can become very intense and interactive, children do not like leaving them abruptly. If they know they have only 15 to 30 minutes to end their session, they can plan to cease playing after completing a mission or task without starting a new one. However, kids who are too young or unable to budget their time may not benefit from a "15- to 30-minute warning signal." If a transition time does not work well with your child after two or three attempts, consider applying set gaming times. For example, you may state your child can only game between 7 and 9 p.m. and not during the hour right before dinner, if that is the time when arguments most often take place.

It can also be helpful to ensure that no gaming occurs in the hour or two before bedtime. This is a time kids often fall into the trap of wanting to keep playing "just a little bit longer." Many families successfully institute a no-gaming policy after 9 or 10 at night, and extending this rule to the use of all electronic devices, or Internet activities, can be beneficial.

3. In designing your rules, consider a reasonable time frame for reassessment. You can follow your plan for 1 or 2 months and then reevaluate it. Instituting a temporary change will result in greater buy-in than a permanent change. You may decide that the initial plan is too restrictive. You could then loosen it after a couple of months if your child is adhering to it and no problems are evident. Remember that it is easier to loosen restrictions than to tighten them. Therefore, for young children or adolescents, you probably do not want to impose initial rules that are similar to current levels of play and then try to reduce the amount of play gradually over time. Your child may perceive more restrictive plans as undue punishment, especially if subsequent plans allow for less playing time. You do not want to be punishing your child for abiding by your rules!

4. Determine a realistic consequence for breaking the rules. The outcome for violating the rules must be enforceable and immediately applicable. You do not want to tell your 14-year-old child she cannot get her driver's permit when she is 16 if she breaks the rules next week. A more reasonable option is a complete ban on gaming (or media use more generally) for several days or weeks if she does not abide by the rules. A more severe consequence may be elimination of the device(s) completely. However, do not threaten a consequence that you (and your partner, if applicable) are not willing to follow through with.

5. As a parent of a minor, you have every right—and a responsibility—to ensure that you know and approve of which game(s) your child is playing. Know what games your child is playing. Ask him directly or view web browsers if you are unsure. Find out about his preferred games.

In addition to setting rules about times for playing, you should also include rules related to the types of games allowed. Entertainment Software Rating Boards (ESRB) for video games are available at http://www.esrb.org/ratings/search.aspx. In Europe, the Pan European Game Information (PEGI) is a parallel system that rates gaming systems. Its site is available at http://www.pegi. info/en/index. You should review the type and content of the games your child is playing on these or other sites. If you do not know the games your child plays, you can ask or review browser histories (see Box 8.1 in this chapter). You can and should prevent purchase and use of games with extreme violence or graphic sexual content. In particular, given concerns about MMORPGs, consider disallowing use of these games entirely among children and young adolescents. In designing your rules, specify that you will not only monitor the time spent gaming but also the specific types of games. For example, you could allow use of games with an ESRB rating of appropriate for "Everyone" or "Teens," but not MMORPGs or any games with violent content.

6. Finally and importantly, once you have established your rules, you must consistently monitor and apply them. You cannot allow your child to bend the rules when you are tired or distracted. You cannot apply the rules differently if your child feels ill or does not have any homework one day. Regardless of other issues that arise, you need to follow through with the consequences *immediately* if your child breaks the rules. You must feel comfortable with the plan you propose, and you must be committed, willing, and able to follow through with it. If both parents are involved, both must be on board with the monitoring of gaming time and rules surrounding it. As noted earlier, you should include a time frame for the plan. Rules can be reevaluated after you and your child gain some experience with them. Chapter 7 outlined response styles and communication tips that can assist you in implementing your plan proactively and assertively.

In particular, consider how you can enforce and ensure limits. As mentioned earlier in this chapter, computers, televisions, and gaming devices (even smartphones) should not be allowed in children's bedrooms.[10] Moving devices to central areas of the home allows for social controls over their use. It also ensures you can review and regulate the amounts of time your child spends gaming and the types of games he or she is playing.

Consider using "Parental control" settings as well. These are available on newer gaming consoles. For example, the Xbox has a family timer that will shut off the game after a specific time of use elapses. Password-protected parental controls are also available on computers, although they can vary considerably depending on operating systems and games. You can look up instructions online, stop at your local computer store, or call the game's or device's customer support line for instructions about parental controls on specific equipment and games. You should invest the time needed into setting these controls to assist you in enforcing rules related to playing times. Whether it is you alone, you and your partner together, or you in conjunction with technology controls, you need to be consistent and thorough in your decisions about gaming rules. If you need more support through the process or if you and your partner disagree on the extent of the problems or methods for addressing them, consider speaking with a family therapist. Chapter 7 provided examples about how to communicate assertively with your child about game playing and other issues more generally. These skills can also be useful for discussions with current and former partners and other family members.

Let's return to the case of Pete, Amy, and their son, Sam, who plays video games on his computer and an Xbox. The Xbox is at his mother's house, so he can only play that there, but he also spends most of his time there. Before his parents had instituted any rules about gaming, Sam's parents each tracked his gaming time for 2 weeks using Worksheet 8.2. They determined he played about 23 hours one week and 28 hours the next, when they added the time he spent gaming during the weekend at his father's house. After reviewing these records and discussing what they thought was reasonable, his parents compromised and decided that he can play, but for no more than 7 hours a week in total. They do not want him playing more than 45 minutes a day on Mondays through Thursdays, and a maximum of 2 hours a day on Fridays, weekends, and school holidays. All gaming, and Internet use, must stop by 10 p.m. His father wants at least one day a week with no video game playing. His play on school days can occur only after Sam shows his parent his completed homework assignments, and on Saturdays and Sundays once he finishes household chores. He can only play games rated appropriate for "Everyone" on ESRB.

Sam's mother may decide to keep the Xbox (or detachable plugs or control units) locked in a closet or a safe in her bedroom. She will now put on a timer for 45 to 120 minutes (depending on the day) when he requests to play and has fulfilled his other responsibilities. When the timer goes off, he must relinquish the game.

With this plan, Sam can only use the Xbox when his mother is home and she gives it to him, and she closely monitors his duration of play. Sam cannot exceed these limits on the Xbox, given this arrangement. He cannot play while his mother is at work. Playing on a computer may be more difficult to regulate if Sam also uses it for schoolwork. If the computer is relocated to a central area of both homes where either parent can carefully watch what he is doing with it, Sam will no longer be able to play games excessively on it. His father could also use a timer to monitor gaming at his house. The consequence of exceeding the limits or playing without requesting to play is defined as a 1-week loss of the Xbox and no use of the computer except for monitored school use. If practiced with diligence, this plan would clearly prevent excessive game playing in children and young adolescents. This sample contract is shown in Worksheet 8.3, and a blank template appears in Worksheet 8.4.

Of course, Sam may protest this new arrangement. He may act out, refusing to do any homework unless he can play more. He may even threaten to hurt himself or to run away. Even in these cases, it is important for Sam's parents to remain firm about reasonable limits. If his reactions are extreme, you can remind him that he can still play, but there are limits. You can discuss that the new plan will be in place for a 1-month period. You can reassure your child that you will reconsider the daily or weekly limits if he abides by them over the next month. As you are recording game playing under these new guidelines, simultaneously introduce replacement activities during former common gaming times (see Chapter 9). Reward non-game-playing behaviors (see Chapter 10). When you develop and institute clear rules assertively, you will find that both you and your child can succeed!

Worksheet 8.3
Sample game-playing contract for children and younger adolescents

I agree to play only the following video games: _those rated as appropriate for "Everyone" and "Everyone 10+," such as Star Wars Racer Revenge and sports games._

I agree to NOT play any video games until I have: _completed my homework and cleaned my room. I will not play games after 10 pm at night._

For the next _4_ weeks, I will play video games no more than _45_ minutes per day on _Mondays through Thursdays, which are school nights._

On _Fridays, weekends, and school holidays,_ I will not play more than _120_ minutes per day.

In total, I will not play more than _7_ hours throughout the week, and I will not play any games on at least _1_ day each week.

My father agrees to monitor and to let me play video games under these conditions for the next _4_ weeks. I understand that if I do not follow these rules, I will lose access to all game-playing devices _(including my smartphone)_ for _1_ week. If I adhere to these rules until _3 / 4 / 2018_, we will reassess goals at that time.

Sam	_2 / 4 / 2018_
Signature	Date

Dad	_2 / 4 / 2018_
Signature of witness	Date

Mom	_2 / 4 / 2018_
Signature of witness	Date

Worksheet 8.4
Game-playing contract for children and younger adolescents

I agree to play only the following video games:_____.

I agree to NOT play any video games until I have:_____

_____

For the next _____ weeks, I will play video games no more than _____ minutes

per day on _____.

(list specific days here)

On _____, I will not play more

(list specific days here)

than _____ minutes per day.

In total, I will not play more than _____ hours throughout the week, and I will
not play any games on at least _____ days each week.

My parent agrees to let me play video games under these conditions for the
next _____ weeks. I understand that if I do not follow these rules, I will lose access to all game-playing devices for _____ week(s). If I adhere to these rules until
_____ / _____ / _____, we will reassess goals at that time.

_____   _____

Signature   Date

_____   _____

Signature of witness   Date

Negotiating reasonable limits for older adolescents and adults

If your child is an older adolescent or you are concerned about an adult child, you may be unable to restrict access to gaming devices or enforce limits. However, you can still discuss the current level of gaming and whether any reductions in time may be preferred. Simply recognizing the extent of a behavior can have a major impact upon reducing it. An adolescent who has not yet experienced significant negative consequences such as Tim may, upon reflection, realize that he is spending more time than he intended gaming. This realization may serve as an initial impetus to change. Although Tim may not have admitted it overtly, he may have received a failing or near-failing grade on an exam or homework assignments, which he may have attributed at least in part to a late-night gaming episode.

To facilitate commitment to change, especially among older adolescents and adults, you can ask how much your child would *like* to be gaming. Directly inquiring about the optimal amount of time to be spent gaming each day or week can stimulate important self-discoveries. Some adolescents and young adults may say they like and want to be able to play games every day and for multiple hours per day. However, they might recognize they have fallen into a trap that whenever they start to play they feel they cannot stop. Chapter 3 notes that a common concern among gamers themselves is that they spend more time than they intended gaming.

Returning to the case of Tim, if he refused the idea of limiting his gaming to certain nights or stopping play at a particular time, his mother could try another angle. She might say,

"Okay, I see how that might be difficult to do. What do you think would be reasonable then? How much gaming is ideal, and how much do you think is too much? I'm sure that on some days or weeks you do regret how much time you've played. How much did you play the last time you regretted it?"

Once Tim admits to an amount that is too much, something below that level should be considered an upper limit. For example, if he replies,

> *"Well, last night I played for about 6 hours straight. That was too much. I wished I had stopped sooner. I just lost track of time."*

His mother may then respond,

> *"Okay, that is a start then. Six hours in a day does seem like too much. I also presume you wouldn't want to play up to 6 hours every day. How many days a week would you feel okay about playing up to 6 hours, or why don't we say 5 hours, as you just said 6 is too much. If you played up to 5 hours a day, 7 days a week, that would be 35 hours a week. That is even more than you said you played this past week. Is 25 hours a week a level you'd be okay with trying to stay under—no more than 5 hours a day, and no more than 25 hours a week?"*

Because this is right within the range at which he already admits to playing, it would be unlikely that Tim would dispute this as a reasonable upper limit of playing time.

As noted earlier, people without Internet gaming disorder generally play less than daily and less than 12 hours a week. Few young adults with mild to moderate symptoms of gaming disorder, however, will agree to this low level, especially if they have been playing at much greater rates. Their proposal may be to continue gaming whenever they feel like it, but not exceed the level that they admit to gaming. If so, make a commitment with them to try to stick to their current level, just for a week. A written contract regarding the desired maximum frequency and extent of gaming can help. Worksheet 8.5 shows a sample contract for an older adolescent or adult child.

Although Tim's mother is not happy about her son gaming 25 hours a week, she realizes that 25 hours a week is actually *less* than he has been gaming. She might say,

Worksheet 8.5
Tim's sample game-playing contract

For the next week, I agree to play games no more than __5__ hours per day on any day of the week.

In total, I will not play more than __25__ hours throughout the week.

_____*Tim*_____	_____*10/4/2017*_____
Signature	Date
_____*Mom*_____	_____*10/4/2017*_____
Signature of witness	Date

"Let's try this for a week. Keep track of how often you are playing just like you did last week. Let's see if at the end of the week it is no more than 5 hours a day and no more than 25 hours a week. If you are honest with yourself about how much you are playing and you can keep under those levels without having problems, that is my goal too. Let's just write that down so we both remember what we talked about in terms of upper limits."

Over the course of the next few weeks, encourage your child to record each day whether he played any video games and, if so, for how long. Although you can continue to monitor gaming independently, this phase involves encouraging your child to keep his or her own records as well. This process will allow self-discovery about days on which he was and was not successful in maintaining limits. At the end of the week, any days that gaming did not exceed limits can be distinguished from those that did. A good understanding of the patterning of gaming, especially excessive gaming, is critical for reducing it.

If the original goals are not very ambitious, as in Tim's case, you are still working together—as opposed to apart—on the process. Getting Tim to monitor accurately his own gaming is important for his learning to recognize when it is too much. Over the course of the next week, he may realize that he does spend more than 5 hours a day several days per week gaming. He may also begin to acknowledge that he is regretting his playing more often than he initially admitted. By self-recording his own gaming, he can begin to learn to regulate it.

Tim was willing to assess how much he was playing. It is possible that your child may refuse to participate in this process or may do so in an insincere manner, grossly underestimating how much he plays. If your child will not keep handwritten logs but will discuss with you his gaming times daily, then you can take ownership of the monitoring logs. Review them with him regularly using a caring and assertive, but not aggressive, tone. If even these discussions are counterproductive, then you can continue with your own independent recording logs.

The more you are able to institute these suggestions and changes, including the recording, the greater the likelihood that your child's gaming will decrease. As noted earlier, however, you need not undertake all these recommendations, and you need not institute them all at once. If your child or even you yourself cannot record gaming times regularly, you can still help reduce your child's gaming by enacting the steps in the next two chapters.

9

Step 2—Replace: Finding healthy recreational activities

Pete and Amy learned a lot by recording their son's gaming. Pete realized that Sam gamed even more at his house than at his mother's, at least on the weekend he was with him. Amy, who was originally in some denial about the extent of Sam's gaming, came to see how much her son really was playing. They had set forth clear rules about gaming, but what was Sam going to do to fill his time if he was no longer gaming over 20 hours a week?

By recording gaming behavior for several weeks, as Chapter 8 outlines, you will have a better understanding of your child's typical gaming patterns. If both parents are recording gaming, you will have two perspectives. If your child is old enough and willing to monitor his own gaming independently, the process of self-recording is likely to lead to reduced gaming on its own. Even if your child will not participate in the process, once you recognize how and when your child plays, you will be in a much better position to modify these patterns and, ultimately, minimize harm from them.

Replacing gaming with other activities is critical to changing this behavior. Your child is gaming in large part because she finds it fun and it is something she is good at. Gaming can be done virtually any time, with little planning or effort. All it requires is turning on a device—it's nearly instantaneous. Because many devices are used for other activities in addition to gaming, it's even easier to fall into the trap. While surfing the Internet or checking texts or social media, a game is just one click—and one second—away. When your child has little else to do, games are always there to fill the time.

Identifying other recreational activities

To help your child fill free time, actively promote participation in other recreational activities.[1] For kids who used to take part in sports or other activities but no longer do, find ways to reinvolve them. If there are activities they have always wanted to try, you can help them to join a club or go on outings. For kids with difficulties in social situations, encourage activities that can be done on a solitary basis as well as social ones that will not be overwhelming. Consider activities that you and other family members can do with your child.

Remember that gaming occupies a lot of time—in many cases 20 or more hours per week. These hours *need* to be filled with other activities if the gaming is to decrease. Therefore, it is important to identify and encourage hobbies that your child enjoys and that are incompatible with gaming. These should be activities unrelated to Internet use. The more rewarding other nonelectronic pastimes become, the less tempted your child will be to game. The replacement of activities should be on the days of the week and during the times of the day when your child most often plays video games.

Pete realized that Sam gamed for hours each weekend when he was at his house, but Pete rarely planned things for them to do on these days. Pete always meant to spend more quality time with his son, but other things always seemed to get in the way. Weekends were often filled with errands and other household tasks he needed to get done. In whatever time was left over, Pete just wanted to relax on the weekend, and he did so by watching sports on the television. When Sam was younger he used to watch with his dad, but he seemed to have lost interest in sports over the years. Pete began to realize that his own relaxation on the weekends was perpetuating his son's gaming.

Use Worksheet 9.1 to consider other activities your child may enjoy. This worksheet lists a range of leisure activities on the first page. Being as inclusive as possible, check off anything that your child enjoys doing now, did in the past, or may consider trying in the future. List other things that are not on the list but that he may find fun. You can also return to your recording logs (as discussed in Chapter 8) and look for activities that your child was doing when not gaming.

The goal here is to brainstorm and come up with a variety of possibilities. The wider the selection of options, the more likely it is that your child will participate in some of them. The more activities he tries, the greater is the likelihood that he will find one (or more) to do regularly. The more activities your child engages in, the less time he will spend gaming. This exercise may appear somewhat simple on the surface, but it is very important because integrating more recreational activities into your child's life may hold the key to decreasing gaming in the short term and long run.

In terms of things that his son may like, Pete may check off going to sports games, listening to music, watching television, going to movies, hiking, going to the ocean, and boating. He may also indicate skiing, playing board games and chess, solving puzzles, and going to museums, even though they hadn't done those in a very long time. He knows his son likes to play laser tag and read comic books, so he adds those to the "other" category. He is also sure his son would love to try skydiving and motorcycling, although he certainly wouldn't condone these last two.

Once you identify a large number of alternate activities, rank them from 1 to 10, in the order you think your child will most enjoy. Try not to impose your preferences on your child. This worksheet gets at activities *your child* may or will find fun. Even if his favorite might be something totally impractical, like skydiving, list the ones you think he would like best.

Although you should complete this exercise on behalf of your child, you may also want to involve him in it. Using a blank version

Worksheet 9.1
Identifying enjoyable activities

Every day should include at least one fun activity.

The more the better!

Below, check activities that your child may find fun or enjoyable.

- ☐ Being in the country.
- ☐ Talking about sports.
- ☐ Meeting new people.
- ☐ Going to a concert.
- ☐ Playing baseball or softball.
- ☐ Planning trips or vacations.
- ☐ Being at the beach.
- ☐ Doing artwork or crafts.
- ☐ Rock or mountain climbing.
- ☐ Reading books.
- ☐ Playing golf.
- ☐ Rearranging/decorating a room.
- ☐ Going to a sports event.
- ☐ Reading "How To" books.

- ☐ Going to service or social club meetings.
- ☐ Going to community events.
- ☐ Snow skiing.
- ☐ Acting.
- ☐ Being with friends.
- ☐ Being in a big city.
- ☐ Playing pool or billiards.
- ☐ Being with children.
- ☐ Playing chess or checkers.
- ☐ Designing or crafting.
- ☐ Visiting people.
- ☐ Bowling.
- ☐ Gardening.
- ☐ Dancing.
- ☐ Sitting in the sun.
- ☐ Riding a motorcycle.
- ☐ Just sitting and thinking.
- ☐ Going to fairs, carnivals, or amusement parks.
- ☐ Talking about religion, philosophy, or politics.

- ☐ Meditating, doing yoga.
- ☐ Playing board games (Monopoly, Scrabble).
- ☐ Reading the newspaper or magazines.
- ☐ Swimming.
- ☐ Running or jogging.
- ☐ Listening to music.
- ☐ Knitting, crocheting, needlework.
- ☐ Going to the library.
- ☐ Watching people.
- ☐ Repairing things.
- ☐ Bicycling.
- ☐ Writing letters, cards, notes.
- ☐ Caring for houseplants.
- ☐ Taking a walk.
- ☐ Playing sports.

List other ideas of fun things:

_____

_____

☐ Reading short stories or poems.
☐ Going to lectures or hearing speakers.
☐ Playing musical instruments.
☐ Boating (canoeing, sailing, motorboats).
☐ Camping.
☐ Working in politics.
☐ Working on cars, bikes, etc.
☐ Solving problems, puzzles, crosswords.
☐ Having lunch with friends.
☐ Playing tennis.
☐ Taking a relaxing, hot shower or bath.
☐ Woodworking, carpentry.
☐ Writing stories, plays, or poems.
☐ Exploring (hiking, cave exploring).
☐ Having a conversation.
☐ Singing in a group.
☐ Going to church functions.
☐ Watching television.
☐ Watching sports.
☐ Cooking.

☐ Having friends come visit.
☐ Playing in a sports competition.
☐ Getting massages, backrubs, or manicures.
☐ Going to a park or picnic.
☐ Photography.
☐ Gathering objects (shells, leaves, flowers, stamps).
☐ Helping someone.
☐ Being in the mountains.
☐ Meeting new people.
☐ Eating good meals.
☐ Wrestling or boxing.
☐ Going to a museum or exhibit.
☐ Going to a health club.
☐ Being with family.
☐ Horseback riding.
☐ Talking on the phone.
☐ Going to movies.
☐ Coaching someone.
☐ Writing in a diary.
☐ Playing football.

Top Ten Fun Activities

1. _____
2. _____
3. _____
4. _____
5. _____
6. _____
7. _____
8. _____
9. _____
10. _____

of Worksheet 9.1, ask him to check the activities he would like to try. How many of his preferences matched your ideas of things he may enjoy? How many additional things did he indicate may be fun? Would he consider trying any activities that you checked and he didn't? Did you learn anything new about your child by working on this exercise?

After determining desirable activities, Worksheet 9.2 classifies them into categories. These groupings will help you think about the types of activities you could introduce at particular times and situations. Your child may also have ideas about which activities would be most enjoyable at different times.

Categorizing recreational activities

At the top of Worksheet 9.2, consider all the activities your child does at least occasionally. Then, list those that he has not done in a very long time.

Next, consider activities that generally need to be planned in advance. These may be those that require prepaid tickets or reservations or are fairly expensive. They may also require the involvement of another person.

After noting planned activities, list in the fourth section some activities that can be done on the spur of the moment. Refer back to activities checked on Worksheet 9.1 to identify at least several that can be done virtually any time with little or no planning or effort.

In the fifth section of Worksheet 9.2, identify some things that can be done for no or very little money. Consider as widely as possible all sorts of fun activities that your child may enjoy doing beyond gaming. The goal is to fill up most, or at least some, of his gaming hours with fun alternatives.

There are also spaces to classify solitary and social activities. Here, divide the activities identified on Worksheet 9.1 into these categories, realizing that they need not be mutually exclusive. For example, watching a sporting event or listening to music can be done alone or with others. For activities that can be social, consider with whom they could be done. Some activities may be best suited for family members, while others are most likely to occur in the company of friends. Still others may lead to the development of new friendships. Be sure to list at least a few examples of each type of that activity your child may enjoy.

In creating these lists, think about the benefits your child may be deriving from gaming. It is not only filling free time, but he may also like the socialization component, the competitive or challenging aspects, or the manner in which games can substitute for real life. As you consider alternate activities, think about how these positive effects of game playing may be accomplished, at least in part, in other contexts. If your child enjoys socializing, focus on in-person activities that involve opportunities for interactions with others. If he likes cognitive challenges and is mathematically inclined, try to come up with other activities that involve similar skill sets, such as competing in Lego building or chess competitions, or even learning to play an instrument. For those who are fulfilling fantasy roles online, participating in acting classes or a community theater production may serve a similar function. Even if your child has never tried and has no interest in being on stage, he may consider working backstage on a theater production. You may not fully understand why your child is so drawn toward gaming, but the more potentially enjoyable alternatives you can suggest, the more likely some of them will replace gaming.

Pete, for example, may recall that years ago he used to take his son hiking at least a couple times a year. They would drive out somewhere and hike up to the top of a mountain or large hill, or sometimes to a cave, valley, or lake. They also used to go fishing occasionally at a nearby river. Pete smiled remembering about some of these past outings with his son. He also remembered they went out to the movies as a family every time Disney released a new movie. He realized he hadn't been to a movie with his son since he was 9 or

Worksheet 9.2
Classifying fun activities

1) Identify enjoyable activities that your child <u>already does</u> on occasion.

Example: Sometimes goes downhill skiing, draws and paints, and dances.

_____ _____ _____

_____ _____ _____

_____ _____ _____

2) Generate ideas about fun things your child <u>has never tried</u> or <u>has not done in a long time</u>.

Example: He may enjoy hiking or cycling. He used to like playing soccer.

_____ _____ _____

_____ _____ _____

_____ _____ _____

3) List enjoyable activities that usually need to be <u>planned in advance</u>.

Example: Going on a weekend trip, going to a concert, playing basketball with friends.

_____ _____ _____

_____ _____ _____

_____ _____ _____

4) Consider activities that can be <u>done spontaneously</u>. These should be activities that require little or no planning or equipment (unless the equipment is readily available at your home, such as art or carpentry tools and supplies).

Example: Listening to music, reading magazines, going for a walk, taking a hot shower.

_____   _____   _____

_____   _____   _____

_____   _____   _____

5) Include enjoyable activities that <u>cost very little or no money</u>.

Example: Going to the library, watching a movie on TV, listening to music, drawing.

_____   _____   _____

_____   _____   _____

_____   _____   _____

6) Select activities that can be done alone, with family members, and with existing friends, and some that may lead to new friendships. Be sure to include at least some of the Top Ten favorites from Worksheet 9.1.

<u>Alone:</u>	<u>With family:</u>	<u>With friends:</u>	<u>New friends:</u>
Listen to music	*Build or fix things*	*Play sports*	*Gym*
Watch TV	*Cook, eat*	*Go to concerts*	*Club meeting*

Alone:	With family:	With friends:	With new friends:
_____	_____	_____	_____
_____	_____	_____	_____
_____	_____	_____	_____

10. He stopped to think about why he hadn't made the time to see a movie or go hiking or fishing with his son in so many years.

Filling high-risk times with other recreational activities

The final aspect of this step is to match alternative activities to times when gaming most often occurs. Worksheet 9.3 asks you to consider the times that your child is most likely to be gaming. These may involve specific days of the week (e.g., weekends) or specific times of the day (e.g., late evenings). By reviewing the recording logs from Chapter 8, you should be able to identify the high-risk times for gaming. After you list those high-risk times, consider two or more alternate activities that your child could do *instead of* gaming at that time. If the high-risk time is one during which no one else will be around, select from solitary activities. If the high-risk time is when family members will be available, consider including relatives who can encourage or participate in the activity. Activities that are best planned in advance should be listed alongside high-risk times when planning is possible, such as weekends.

In the upcoming week, focus on one or two of the high-risk gaming times. Choose times that you will be around and able to suggest alternatives. If you are unable to be home when your child arrives back from school, that is not a good high-risk time to select. If your child typically starts playing right after dinner and you are home then, that may be an ideal time. You may decide to focus initially on nights you know you will be home early. You need not try to address all the high-risk times at once. The goal is to select a couple that will be easiest to interrupt the *initiation* of a gaming episode with an alternate enjoyable activity.

Using some of the activities you already indicated your child will enjoy in Worksheets 9.1 and 9.2, decide on at least two activities that you could suggest and encourage during a few specific high-risk

Worksheet 9.3
Replace high-risk times with other activities

Think about the timing and patterning of typical game playing. List two or more times or days when your child is most likely to play video games in the left column. Use your recording sheets (Worksheet 8.1) to determine high-risk times.

Next, consider the types of other enjoyable activities that could occur during times game playing is most likely. Be sure to include some enjoyable activities that you are certain your child would really enjoy doing (e.g., from the Top Ten list in Worksheet 9.1). List some activities that involve others, and some that are solitary in nature. Be sure to include activities that are realistic substitutes for the high-risk game-playing periods.

Example:

Typical times for playing games: *Alternative activity:*

- *after school*
- *late at night*
- *when bored*
- *when had a bad day*
- *Sunday mornings*

- *make dinner, do a puzzle*
- *watch a movie, read a book or magazine*
- *plan for a weekend skiing trip*
- *write a journal entry, draw, or listen to music*
- *plan a family outing, go on a walk*

Typical times for playing games:

Alternative activities:
(List at least two activities for
each game-playing time):

_____

_____

_____

_____

_____

_____

_____

_____

_____

_____

_____

_____

_____

_____

_____

_____

times. Pete may select a hiking trip for the weekend, or a movie or trip to a local museum as a backup if it rains.

Be sure your choices are feasible, and consider selecting at least one that you are quite certain your child would jump at the chance to do. In other words, select from some of the Top Ten activities that are realistic given the time of day and other situational factors such as resources, weather, etc. Your two choices may be, "Go out for ice cream," or "Rent an on-demand movie." As evening approaches, consider which of these activities you think your child would be more likely to agree to do that night. As dinner is ending, say, "I'm kind of having a craving for ice cream. Do you want to go to Ben and Jerry's tonight?"

Your child probably had no plans for after dinner and was likely to resume gaming. By suggesting something else that you are pretty sure he would enjoy, you are stopping the cycle of gaming, at least for an hour or so. As you return home from the ice cream parlor, you can plant a seed for him to try something else for the remainder of the evening to further decrease the probability that he will turn to gaming that night. You might say,

> "Do you want to go and shoot some hoops tonight? Remember when we used to do that almost every evening in the summer? Let's give it a try! I bet you can't beat your old man."

If you have a younger child whose gaming you are carefully monitoring and limiting (Chapter 8), your child ought to be inclined to try something new during the periods his gaming is restricted. You can present them as ways to take his mind off playing video games.

Even if your child rejects your suggestions of activities, you can learn from this experience. Don't give up! If your proposal is not enticing, you can come up with another more exciting alternative next time. If you suggest things that are more enjoyable, you will find one that beats out another night of gaming. You may need to make suggestions several different times, offering different options. The more you try, the greater the probability your child will choose one.

Remember, too, that what you consider fun may not be consistent with your child's preferences. Ask your child what he would like to do or new activities he would like to try. Add them to the lists in Worksheet 9.2 where appropriate. Have him commit to doing a few and facilitate his getting involved in at least one or two new activities over the upcoming several days.

Pete may resolve to go out on a hiking trip with his son the next weekend that he stays with him. He started researching some nearby hiking trails and printed out the few that looked best. He decided to let Sam choose which one he wanted to go to on the next Saturday they would be together. He also came up with two backup plans in case it rained that weekend. He also found the times and locations for the airing of a popular movie for kids of Sam's age and the hours of opening of a museum they used to go to.

Some high-risk times will be more difficult to address. There are few things that can be done in the middle of the night, and you are not likely to be staying up all night to see if your child is gaming. However, if you are able to replace at least some high-risk times with other activities, you should be decreasing the overall amount of time your child spends gaming. You will also be expanding your child's recreational options. These healthier activities can become rewarding in their own right, just as the gaming did.

Once you come up with a few alternatives to gaming, keep track of them. These are activities or events that you can continue to suggest; they have been successful at least once in the past. As you plan alternatives, keep track of when and how much your child is gaming on Worksheet 8.1, as well as the other activities. When an enjoyable alternate activity occurs during a high-risk time, does your child resume gaming immediately after that activity ends or does he wait a while before playing? Does gaming decrease overall on days that activities outside the house occur? Is gaming lower overall on weeks that more recreational activities take place? Both you and your child may be surprised how much gaming recedes when other fun activities are planned and prioritized.

10

Step 3—Reward: Positive reinforcement for nongaming

Pete was impressed with how much more fun and enjoyable the weekends with his son became when they went out and did things together compared to when they stayed home and inevitably argued over gaming. Pete was no longer seeing gaming as a problem, at least not when his son was with him. They were busy much of the time they spent together, and Pete made sure to plan at least one outing for each of their weekends together. However, he realized that Sam was with his mother most of the time, and she had a harder time organizing special activities, in particular on the weekdays. Amy tried to encourage her son to try out a few new things, especially after-school activities, but Sam still seemed to have hours of unstructured time many afternoons. With a lot of oversight and reminders initially, however, Sam was sticking to the rules about gaming, and Amy was proud of him for it.

Positive reinforcement for not gaming goes beyond replacing the games with other activities. It involves actively rewarding, or reinforcing, alternative behaviors. It entails providing rewards to your child when he or she is involved in activities that do not relate to gaming. These rewards can be tangible, involving actual goods, services, or even money. They can also be intangible, such as verbal praise or simply attention. Step 2 (Replace, Chapter 9) and Step 3 (Reward, this chapter) are not mutually exclusive. You can replace gaming times with rewarding recreational activities, and these activities can also serve as rewards for not gaming.

Your initial reaction to this suggestion of directly rewarding nongaming may be one of hesitation. You may be unsure about what the rewards should be. It is normal to feel somewhat reluctant about providing rewards for not playing video games. It can also feel awkward or artificial. Some parents may even resent the concept of rewarding their child for not doing something that she or he should not be doing anyway.

Giving positive rewards for not playing video games is actually a show of support. When this process is done correctly, it can have powerful effects on changing behavior. It can also improve communication more generally (see Chapter 7). Before you react too quickly about the concept of rewarding your child for not gaming, consider the following. Using rewards or reinforcers is the MOST effective intervention for reducing drug use behavior,[1] and it can be very useful for adolescents.[2] This technique is highly effective in reducing use of alcohol, cigarettes, marijuana, cocaine, opioids, and other addictive substances.[3] Even patients with severe substance use disorders and those with significant mental health problems respond to positive reinforcement.[4] Positive reinforcement techniques are also effective for other health behaviors, such as enhancing weight-loss efforts,[5] increasing exercise,[6] and improving adherence to medications.[7] These techniques are commonplace in schools as well.

Family members can reward many types of behaviors.[8] As family members become accustomed to using positive reward approaches, they feel they are taking better control over their own behaviors. They can experience improved reactions to their loved one's behaviors as well. Remember that you cannot control the behaviors of others, but you can control how you respond to them. Your responses do influence your child's behaviors, in both positive and negative ways.

The goal of this exercise is to positively influence your child's decisions to not play video games, or at least not at harmful levels.

As you become familiar with this process, you will feel better about doing it.

Determining appropriate rewards

Box 10.1 provides tips about selecting rewards for not gaming. Specifically, you should identify things or activities that your child wants and desires. Remember that what he or she likes may not be consistent with what you want or desire. If your son or daughter does not enjoy social activities, you should not be selecting social events as the primary rewards, even if you think they are fun or may be important.

In Worksheet 10.1, brainstorm a list of all conceivable rewards for not gaming. Rewards can include highly desirable things, as well as modest incentives. Thus, it is appropriate to list some moderately expensive potential rewards, especially in the top section of the worksheet. Also consider rewards that you can realistically provide. In other words, a trip to the Bahamas, although highly desired, may not be financially or logistically possible. On the other hand, you need not eliminate all costly rewards. A weekend trip to the beach may be possible to manage once or twice a year as a reward. In section 2 of the worksheet, list a range of feasible rewards.

BOX 10.1. Guide for selecting rewards

1. Think about all the types of things your child wants or likes.
2. Be sure to include a variety of feasible rewards.
3. Consider some intangible rewards.
4. Include other people in some rewards.
5. Integrate rewards that involve participation in recreational activities.

Worksheet 10.1
Rewards

1) Below, generate a list of possible rewards. Be sure to fill all the lines. Add more to the back side if you can. The more rewards the better!

2) Include some smaller rewards, too. Many rewards may not be possible to deliver, and some you may only be able to give once due to their size or cost. Think about some smaller rewards that you could give on more than one occasion. Write down below rewards that might be appreciated repeatedly.

3) Now, consider additional intangible rewards. This means including things that your child may like that do not cost anything or involve goods or services. They may be a pat on the back, a congratulations statement, a card or small note left in a backpack, a phone call or conversation, etc. Write down some intangible things that will make your child happy or smile.

_____   _____

_____   _____

_____   _____

_____   _____

_____   _____

_____   _____

4) Rewards provided by, or done with, others are important too. Think about other people who may be able to do enjoyable things with your child. What kinds of rewards, both tangible and intangible, may others be able to provide or participate in?

_____   _____

_____   _____

_____   _____

_____   _____

_____   _____

_____   _____

_____   _____

5) Recreational activities can be rewards. What fun activities does your child enjoy when he or she is not playing games? What activities might he like to try?

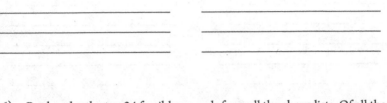

6) Rank order the top 24 feasible rewards from all the above lists. Of all the options listed earlier, first list the reward you think your child would most like and that you will able to provide. Selecting some options from all 5 earlier sections, indicate below 24 rewards that are feasible for you to deliver. List them from most to less preferred in order of preference from your child's perspective.

1. _____
2. _____
3. _____
4. _____
5. _____
6. _____
7. _____
8. _____
9. _____
10. _____
11. _____
12. _____

13. _____
14. _____
15. _____
16. _____
17. _____
18. _____
19. _____
20. _____
21. _____
22. _____
23. _____
24. _____

Finally, above and throughout all the lists in this worksheet, circle rewards that you can give on more than one occasion. These are rewards you can use again and again.

In our example, Amy became sure that the key to reducing Sam's gaming was getting him involved in other activities. She often could not get home from work until late, and after school was a high-risk time for gaming. Even though she kept the Xbox controls locked and away from him, he could play games on the computer when she wasn't home watching, and he spent many days after school alone. Amy knew her son had always wanted to join the ski club at school, but she had always felt it was too expensive. However, she thought this year, because he was maintaining their contract regarding gaming, maybe she could manage to pay for half the fees, if his dad could spring for the other half. This would be a very big reward. Amy also considered smaller rewards, like going to the library to pick out a DVD, a trip to the ice cream parlor, tickets to the movie theater, and iTunes gift cards. He also needed a new pair of sneakers.

The above rewards are all tangible ones. Consider intangible rewards as well. Such rewards may be verbal praise and positive statements, such as, "I'm so glad to see you are doing your homework tonight." Other rewards can involve a congratulatory text message or a card. Some parents post notes on the fridge or on their child's bedroom door or backpack. Amy decided to get a bunch of colored sticky pads that she could write encouraging notes on and leave them in places around the house for Sam to find when he was not gaming. She also thought about texting him more often, just to ask how he was doing or to congratulate him for not gaming; in the past, almost all her texts to him only involved the pragmatics about timing of events or instructing him to do something. She decided that from now on, at least half her texts to him would be simply positive or encouraging in nature. In section 3 of Worksheet 10.1, list some intangible rewards you could use.

Rewards that involve others will expand the pool of options. A visit with a relative can be a reward. A message from a grandmother may be affirming. Reminiscing about old times or reviewing family photos may be enjoyable and rewarding as well. Include possible rewards that involve other people under section 4 of Worksheet 10.1.

Be sure to include rewards that involve recreational pursuits and that take time to do. Going to the movies can be a reward for not gaming. An outing to the movies can easily fill 2 hours, which is 2 hours less of gaming time. If going to the movies is paired with a high-risk time, it can serve as both a replacement and a reward.

Amy realized that her husband had succeeded so well in reducing gaming when Sam was with him because he could so easily fill the limited time with nongaming activities. As Sam was with her at least 4 school nights each week and every other weekend, she needed not only to bear most of the burden of monitoring his gaming, but also to fill much more of his time with other activities. The ski club sounded like one great possibility as it was definitely something Sam wanted, and it would also fill Friday afternoons throughout the winter.

As you contemplate rewards that relate to recreational activities for your child and write them in section 5 of the worksheet, look back on any old gaming logs you completed (Worksheet 8.1). What was your child doing during times he was not gaming? These activities are naturally occurring alternatives to gaming and some can also be construed as rewards for not gaming. Clearly, the recreational and social activities were rewarding to your child if they were substituting for gaming on their own. The rest of this chapter will help you actively and conscientiously employ these fun activities as rewards.

You should come up with a large number of options for rewards throughout Worksheet 10.1. Hopefully, over time, you will be giving out a lot of rewards when your child is not gaming. No one wants the same thing time after time, so variety is key.

As you contemplate possible rewards across all the categories in Worksheet 10.1, remember that anything that involves gaming should not be used as a reward. So, a new video game or a sub-scription to a gaming magazine is not a good choice for a reward. Although this may seem obvious, parents or other well-intentioned family members may choose game-related items as rewards or gifts because they know these are highly desired. Furthermore, some rewards may be intended to be used for nongaming activities, but they may have multiple uses that unintentionally reinforce gaming instead of its absence. An example is purchasing an iPhone or iPad for a teenager. If she can access games on it, its purchase may increase gaming, instead of serving to decrease it.

As a further precaution, try not to confuse rewards with punishment. Allowing your child to go out or stay out late on the weekend (a reward) is different from taking this privilege away (a punishment). Consider a parent who tells her son, "I'm glad to see you aren't playing video games right now. Do you want to use my car to go to the game tonight?" Another may say, "If you play video games, then I'm not going to let you use my car to go to the game tonight." In the first scenario, use of the car becomes a reward for not playing video games. In the second, the teenager is punished for playing. Although parents often use punishment in an attempt to alter their children's behaviors, positive reinforcement can work better. It is also much more pleasant to be on the delivering and receiving end of positive reinforcement!

If your child is gaming at a level that is causing harm, most likely one of the adverse consequences relates to a worsening of relationships. Using positive reinforcement is one way to improve communication and relationships. In contrast, repeatedly punishing your child is likely to perpetuate interpersonal difficulties.

In the last section of Worksheet 10.1, select at least 24 rewards that are feasible for you to deliver and that your child would enjoy. Using suggestions within all 5 earlier sections of this worksheet, select at least 3 to 6 from each section that are desirable and possible to deliver. Identify 24 different possibilities that range from very small intangible (or verbal) rewards to ones that may be more extensive in nature, but are still realistic. Rank order them roughly in terms of your child's preference such that the more highly valued ones come first. Those that are relatively less preferred, although still desired, can be ranked lower. Ultimately, you need not restrict yourself to these 24 rewards, but you should try to include many of these initial top rewards for not gaming as you progress through the other sections in this chapter.

Once you have 24 rewards listed, then go back through all the lists in Worksheet 10.1. Circle the rewards that you can provide more than once. For example, a new pair of sneakers might best be considered a one-time reward, while preparing a favorite dinner can be used again and again. Circling these rewards will help you designate which ones you can apply repeatedly, and which are best reserved for a single use.

Pairing rewards to behaviors

After you have determined a large array of possible rewards, consider how and when you can deliver them. This will help you decide which rewards may be most effective, and which may be most useful, in particular circumstances. Ultimately, you will want to match specific nongaming behaviors with appropriately sized rewards. A short period of nongaming should be met with a smaller or even intangible reward. A long period of nongaming during a particularly high-risk time may best be rewarded with a larger tangible item.

Consider a young child who is usually gaming after dinner, but is not playing on a particular evening. You can write that information under "Pattern" of gaming in Worksheet 10.2. Now, consider an appropriate reward for not gaming in that circumstance. List it in the "Reward" section. An example of a reward for not playing right after dinner may be to suggest ordering an on-demand movie to watch together. A reward related to an entire Saturday without playing may be going to the sporting goods store (ideally right before a high-risk time for gaming on Sunday) to pick out a new basketball.

A way you could practice delivering rewards involves reciting your explanation aloud. You can try it several times until you come up with a manner that sounds natural, and that your child will perceive favorably. You might say something like:

> *"I really like it when you don't run off to the computer right after dinner. What do you say we order an on-demand video tonight? I know I rarely*

Worksheet 10.2
Gaming patterns and rewards

Examine patterns of gaming. Consider how you could immediately, upon discovering that your child is NOT gaming at that time, reward nongame-playing behaviors.

Pattern of game playing	Reward for no game playing	Explanation of action
Example: He usually plays video games after dinner, but doesn't this evening.	Example: Suggest ordering an on-demand movie to watch together.	Example: "I really like it when you don't run off to the computer right after dinner. What do you say we order an online movie? I know I rarely let you do this because it can get expensive, but this is a way of my showing you how much it means to me that you are not playing video games tonight. I miss spending time with you in the evenings and doing things together. What do you say—do you want to pick a movie?"
Example: Sometimes she plays all night. Returned computer to a central spot by 10 pm, and bedroom light went off soon after.	Example: Verbal praise	Example: "Thanks for putting the computer away tonight. I hope you have a good night's sleep. I love you!"

let you do this because it can get expensive, but this is a way of my
showing you how much it means to me that you are not playing video
games tonight. I miss spending time with you in the evenings and doing
things together. What do you say—do you want to pick out a movie?"

Imagine how your child would react to that statement. If you think
he would agree that selecting a movie is a good idea, then you are
prepared to reward nongaming after dinner the next time it happens.
If you fumble with your delivery the first few times and it doesn't
sound right, keep trying until you feel comfortable. As you describe
it, try to make sure that the reward is being tied directly to your
child's behavior of *not* playing video games.

Tips

As you complete this worksheet, it might be helpful to keep a few
things in mind. Consider the following tips (Table 10.1 below
provides a useful summary of these):

1. Be timely with rewards. Reward current behaviors. Rewards
are not negotiations for future behaviors in this context. This
method may be different from what you usually do. You may typically provide a reward after a behavior, such as giving an allow-
ance after doing chores, or money for a good report card. These are
delayed rewards that are based on a number of behaviors occurring.
Although this practice is fine in some circumstances, to change an
ingrained behavior such as daily or almost-daily gaming, you'll need
to reward specific nongaming behaviors *right as they occur.* In other
words, don't say, "That is great you didn't play games last night. If
you don't play all weekend too, then you can use my car next week."
Consider your son's reaction to that statement versus this one, "That
is great you aren't playing games *right now.* Let's do something fun
together so you won't get tempted to play later tonight. Do you want

TABLE 10.1 Tips for delivering rewards

Tip	Examples
Be on time.	*Reward current ongoing behaviors only, not past or future behaviors. Rewards are not conditional on future behaviors. Avoid if-then statements when delivering rewards.*
Be patient.	*It may take some time before you see a high-risk time without any game playing to reward.*
Be certain.	*Only provide rewards when you are sure no game playing was recently occurring.*
Be variable.	*You should reward some nongame-playing behavior, but you need not reward every instance of not playing.*
Be flexible.	*You don't have to limit rewards to nongame-playing behavior. Reward behaviors that are incompatible with gaming, especially if they are occurring during a high-risk time for game playing.*
Be persistent.	*If your reward doesn't work, try again with a more highly desired reward. Don't give up.*
Reward yourself!	*Give yourself a pat on the back each time you reward your child! You are improving your relationship every time you use rewards in these manners.*

to plan our next family vacation? I know it's not for a while, but I picked up a couple of brochures last week, and thought you might want to take a look at them with me." Which approach do you think will be more likely stop gaming for the next several hours?

Try not to barter rewards. "If . . . then . . ." statements are examples of bartering, and people rarely perceive them as rewarding. For example, do not say, "If you don't play video games this afternoon, then you can have dessert." These negotiations are likely to be met with oppositional behavior, such as gaming to defy the parent. Instead, say, "I'm so glad to see you aren't gaming now. Do you want to help me make those brownies you used to like so much?" In this latter case, you are linking the positive behavior (i.e., nongaming behavior that is occurring naturally) to the reward (a highly desired food and an activity with you).

2. Be patient. It may take a while before nongaming behaviors occur on their own. You may be prepared to reward your child, but every time you check, he is playing. Remember that it is better to wait patiently for nongaming than to prematurely or inappropriately provide rewards.

If you prepare to reward your child at the early part of a high-risk time, you may prevent gaming. Rather than waiting until 9 p.m. to reward your child for not playing after dinner, reward him a half-hour after dinner is over, if he is not playing then. However, if he rushes to the computer immediately after dinner every night, maybe even 30 minutes is too long to wait. Consider then providing the reward if he is not playing 15 minutes after dinner.

3. Reward only behaviors you are certain about. In other words, be sure to *not* give rewards while, or soon after, your child is gaming. If you do not know what your child was doing in the last half-hour, you might unintentionally be rewarding him when he is in the middle of a game but on his way to the refrigerator to get something to eat. If you notice your child is rushing off to play right after dinner every single night, you might try to interrupt that pattern by engaging in a lengthy (but not contentious) discussion with him during dinner, or involving him in some activity immediately after dinner. If 15 minutes elapses without his going straight toward the computer, that may be the time to institute the first reward for not playing. At least you will have had the entire dinner period without any gaming, plus 15 minutes after dinner. In total, he may have made it 30 minutes without playing a game that evening, which is longer than he usually goes.

Try *not* to reward stopping gaming. You want to reward not gaming in the first place. Be sure there has been no gaming for a reasonable period of time such as at least a half-hour before you deliver a reward. If you arrive home at 7 p.m. and find your child is not gaming, you may be tempted to reward him. However, if you do not know what he was doing since he came home from school at 3 p.m., a reward at 7 p.m. may be rewarding a nearly 4-hour gaming episode!

4. You need not reward every instance, or every moment, of not gaming. You cannot determine what your child is doing throughout the entire day, and you will run out of rewards if you provide one every hour he is not gaming. Balance the rewards with your ability to monitor behavior. Try to provide rewards as often as you reasonably can, and ideally at least a few times a week, or daily. On the other hand, if you reward nongaming several times per day, you may quickly exhaust your list of tangible rewards. You can, however, verbally praise your child at any time, and for any reason!

Although consistent and frequent rewards are the key to changing behavior initially, it's more effective to use rewards variably to maintain long-term change.[9] Once gaming becomes less regular, you can begin reducing the frequency of rewards over time. However, you do not want to go too long between rewards. If you haven't rewarded or acknowledged your child's nongaming behaviors in several weeks, he may feel you are no longer interested in whether he is playing or not. Gaming may be more likely to resume. A general rule of thumb is to try to reward your child at least a few times per week, and up to a couple of times per day in the beginning. Over time, and if gaming is decreasing, rewards of once or twice per week may be sufficient to maintain progress, especially after your child successfully develops a new lifestyle.

5. Be flexible, and reward behaviors that are incompatible with gaming. Reward doing homework, cleaning up after dinner, washing the car, etc. Reward these behaviors especially when they are occurring during times that your child normally plays video games. Even if your child stops gaming, you can continue using this approach to reward other positive behaviors. It'll be good practice for you, and you'll be more comfortable doing it. Find something good your child does each day and reward it—verbally or tangibly!

6. Don't give up. If a reward doesn't work, it is likely because your child did not perceive it as a reward. Try again using a reward that is more likely to be highly valued. If you are sure it is something your child would normally desire, consider different ways of approaching the situation. Rewards need to be desired, or by definition they are not rewards. The more you practice giving rewards, the more rewarding the process will be for you too.

7. Reward yourself as well. Change is never easy. You are trying to change not only your own behavior, but that of your child as well. Whenever your child is not gaming, that is a success not only for your child, but also for you. If an alternate activity substitutes for gaming, you have made an important stride. Each time you reward your child for something he has done well, whether it is a small step or a major achievement, you have done something right. Whenever you are using assertive communication skills, you are making a positive impression on your child. In addition to the tangible and intangible rewards you are providing to your child, think about some you can provide yourself. For an intangible reward, each day before bedtime reflect back and think about what you feel most proud about having done that day. Consider also arranging rewards for yourself—a night out with an old friend, a long bath, or an evening at a show. The more you integrate positive rewards and activities into your own life, the easier it will become to do so with your child as well. As your child witnesses you having a more balanced lifestyle, he may begin to model this behavior.

Putting rewards into action

After considering these suggestions, think about the most likely times and situations in which you may want to reward your child for not gaming in the near future. Practice role-playing, giving the reward with your spouse, a friend, or in front of a mirror.

Amy, in our example, practiced how she was going to tell her son about the big reward of ski club, after confirming with her ex-husband that he would help pay for it. She first tried in front of the mirror, stating,

> *"Sam, your dad and I are proud of you for sticking to our gaming contract for the past few months. We decided we are going to pay for you to join ski club this winter if you continue sticking to the gaming rules. We know you always wanted to try it, and we think you deserve it!"*

After wording her explanation in this manner, Amy realized that one of her statements sounded like a negotiation rather than a reward: she indicated that Sam needed to continue sticking to the gaming rules for them to pay for the ski club. She rethought this aspect of her plan. Was she going to take ski trips away from him if he violated the gaming rules? She decided this type of threat was not necessary and would take away the rewarding aspect. If he violated the gaming contract, she already had contingencies that would apply—she would take away all gaming devices for a week. She tried a slightly different approach:

> *"Sam, your dad and I are proud of you for sticking to our gaming contract for the past few months. We decided we are going to pay for you to join ski club this winter. We know you always wanted to try it, and we think you deserve it! We hope you will love it!"*

Stated in this manner, Amy was delivering a reward. The reward would be a big one, and highly valued. It matched the behavior in that Sam had followed the gaming rules for a long time to achieve it. It was an ideal reward in the sense that it would also reduce any desire for Sam to game for an additional day each week during winter months, when it was more difficult to find enjoyable alternatives to gaming.

In addition to describing large, as well as smaller, rewards to your child, you should also role-play an attempt to use positive reinforcement in which your child may become defensive or even hostile. Your child might yell that you are trying to control him, or that he doesn't want anything you give him. If the conversation becomes heated, it is clearly not rewarding and likely counterproductive. Stop the discussion if your child gets irritated. If the rewards are not genuine or seem superficial, you should reevaluate them. There may be another reward you can use, or a different way to approach delivering it. Review Chapter 7 for more communication tips.

Although practicing may feel silly, it is a crucial part of developing new skills. Remember to be nonconfrontational and supportive. If the conversation does not end up going as you intended, back down and try to end it on a good note. In these cases, it might be best to close the conversation with something like,

"I'm sorry that I offended you. That was the last thing I wanted to do. I really do think it's great that you weren't gaming this evening. I want to support you in that decision, so please let me know what I can do that will help."

Summary

Rewards can be powerfully effective in changing behaviors, but most parents won't be comfortable giving them initially. Changing how you respond to your child may be as hard as it is for your child to reduce gaming. The more you are committed to and practice this approach, the greater the likelihood that it will work. The more you can reward nongaming, the more you will be supporting your child, and minimizing his or her gaming.

11

Extreme cases

What to do if nothing seems to work, or if your child needs a complete ban from gaming

Pete and Amy felt lucky that their son was responding so well to the new gaming rules as well as their changes in lifestyle. Sam was sticking to the contract, never playing after 9 p.m., and not exceeding the daily limits. He almost never gamed anymore at his dad's house, and his mom was beginning to feel like she didn't even need to remind him when it was time to relinquish the games. He used a timer on his cell phone and now stopped games before dinner and prior to reaching his daily limits. On many days, Sam didn't even game at all. Amy liked creating sticky notes with positive phrases for her son, and she left them in his backpack and around the house. She also made sure she texted him at least once a day with encouraging phrases like, "I'm so proud of how hard you studied for your test last night. I hope it went well!" and "That was awesome you went 3 days in a row without any gaming!" Sam was excited to join the ski club, and his dad even bought him a new pair of skis. Pete and Amy, although divorced for several years, felt much better about their own relationship as well. For the first time since the divorce they felt like they were parenting together, and they felt encouraged about their son's future.

Other parents, however, may not be experiencing changes so rapidly or completely. Molly had autism, ADHD, and learning difficulties. She had few friends, and gaming appeared to be her only source of success and fulfillment. Although her mother attempted to

*institute rules about gaming, Molly kept breaking them. Her mom
was regularly removing gaming devices from the home for a week or
more at a time and trying to restrict use of the computer, but Molly
always seemed to fall back into old traps of excessive gaming. She
rarely ended a game without a shouting match. Due to her social
issues and mental health problems, Molly's mom seemed to be having
a difficult time getting her interested in new activities. They were
arguing as much as ever, and Molly's mother was becoming even
more worried about her daughter.*

For many parents, the examples and exercises in this book will be
sufficient to prevent or reduce problems with their child's gaming,
as was the case with Sam's parents. For parents of children with severe gaming problems or those with other significant psychological
or developmental concerns, professional help may also be necessary, as in the case of Molly. If you have actively implemented the
strategies in Chapters 7 through 10 but are not seeing improvements
after 2 or 3 months, then you may also want to consider professional
assistance.

Professional treatment

As Chapter 6 described, you should consult a professional if you
think your child has another mental health condition. ADHD, depression, anxiety, and other disorders may occur alongside Internet
gaming disorder. These conditions can improve with medication
and/or psychotherapy. A psychiatrist will be able to diagnose other
mental health problems and prescribe medications if needed. Other
mental health providers, such as psychologists, social workers, and
counselors, can also assess symptoms, make diagnoses, and provide
therapy. Once the other condition is treated, you may find it easier
to address the gaming problems.

Many families of children with mental health conditions can also benefit from family therapy. Family therapists can help parents, children, and siblings better understand the condition and cope with it. They can also assist in improving family dynamics. Chapter 7 discusses communication skills, but if those aren't enough, a professional can uncover other deep-seated issues. A family therapist will be able to suggest solutions and methods to address concerns specific to your family. It is likely that there are underlying issues affecting gaming as well as family relationships more generally.

Some parents are reluctant to seek professional services for themselves because they believe the problem rests primarily with their child. However, if your child sees that you are willing to change by joining in therapy, he might be more likely to participate as well. This book similarly focuses on ways *your* behaviors impact your child's gaming. The ultimate goal is to decrease gaming, and this is most likely if you both change together or in parallel.

Parents might be hesitant to seek help because they think therapy will be long term. However, some issues can be resolved in relatively short periods of time. Many therapists specialize in time-limited therapy, consisting of as few as 4 to 8 sessions. If you or your child is interested in short-term therapy, it is best to discuss this desire upfront with the provider. Then, all parties will be aware of the period over which progress is expected. After the sessions end, you can reevaluate progress and goals. You can then decide whether or not you want to continue with therapy.

Choosing a therapist is also an important process. It is a good idea to obtain referrals from trusted pediatricians, physicians, or other professionals such as school counselors. Some clinicians, especially in large practices, primarily conduct assessments, but do not provide therapy. Therefore, you should ask directly if you will be seeing the same person for therapy as you do for the assessment. If you attend an initial appointment or therapy session and do not feel comfortable with the provider, you should not feel compelled to continue treatment at that practice. Unless you live in a very rural area, there should be multiple providers from which you can select. Choose one with whom you and your child feel comfortable talking.

In addition to considering professional therapy, you may need to take some more extreme approaches toward addressing your child's gaming problems if they are severe. These include complete abstinence from gaming in the home (giving it up completely), or a less severe method of a gaming "holiday."

Complete abstinence

Some earlier chapters in this book alluded to complete abstinence from gaming. This is an extreme approach, but it can be effective, so long as abstinence can be ensured. The treatment camps in Asia and residential Internet addiction treatment centers in the United States institute complete abstinence from technology during the initial stages of care. Thus, computers, smartphones, and Internet access are not permitted in these settings.

Prohibiting access to gaming technology is easier in a controlled environment than in your own home. To ensure that your child cannot access games at home, you can remove all gaming devices completely. You can also disconnect Internet services. As Chapter 8 notes, this decision entails a real commitment from all family members. It may also greatly inconvenience you and your entire family. Nevertheless, it may be a move you are willing to make if problems are pronounced. Without any access to gaming devices or the Internet, clearly gaming will stop, at least while your child is at home. After professional consultation, Molly's mother might make the decision to eliminate all gaming devices other than a laptop computer and also discontinue the Internet. From now on, she would take Molly to the public library after school to do homework that requires Internet access. When they are home, Molly will be unable to game anymore.

Care should be taken to ensure that gaming outside the home does not replace gaming at home. In other words, if your child starts going to a friend's house 30 hours a week, then he could be replacing home gaming with gaming elsewhere. To prevent this problem, you may need to institute and enforce rules on times away from home if appropriate for the age of your child. You may have to contact your child's friends' parents to make them aware of the situation. You should inform them of your wishes regarding no gaming.

If your child is an adult, you cannot control his whereabouts, but you can stop enabling him to play. If you are providing financial assistance for living expenses directly or indirectly (i.e., not charging for room and board), taking away this support may encourage your child to get a job. Getting a job will allow for more disposable income, but he will then be responsible for allocating his income. He might spend it on gaming, but that is less likely if you are not covering his necessities. He'll have less time for gaming because he'll be working. Charging your child for room and board will also reduce his expendable income so there is less left over for gaming. If you feel uncomfortable having your child pay to live in your home, you can consider placing the room and board he pays you in a bank account. Someday, when you feel he is ready, you can return the money to him, with interest. Whatever resentment he may feel now will eventually be replaced by gratitude.

If you eliminate all potential to game in your own home, your child's gaming will decrease, even if she plays occasionally outside the home. The lack of gaming at home should be enough to initiate other positive changes. Once your child begins to experience home life without being totally wrapped up in video games, she will begin to do other things while at home. She might start exercising or cooking. She might resort to watching more television, but even that might be better than gaming excessively. The time that used to be devoted to gaming has to be directed toward other activities whenever she is home. Once these other activities become ingrained, problems with gaming will dissipate.

Chapter 9 provides useful tips to encourage participation in other activities. It will be easier to replace gaming with other activities and reward nonplaying behaviors if gaming is not possible at home.

A "holiday" from gaming

A less extreme approach than eliminating the Internet and removing all gaming devices entirely is a "gaming holiday." This refers to setting a discrete period of time during which no gaming will occur. It should be for at least a few weeks to allow your child to become accustomed to life without gaming. Once your child learns to live without gaming, he or she can better recognize the problems that gaming created.

Ideally, a gaming holiday will be an agreed-upon approach to minimizing problems. If your child (especially an older child) admits that gaming has become problematic, you might say,

"I am glad to hear that you recognize that gaming is causing problems. For many types of problem behaviors, the best approach is to take a break from them for a bit. If you decide to not play any games at all for a while, you will be in a better position to see how your life is going and if your coursework is improving. You might also sleep better. After the break, you can decide if you want to resume gaming at some level lower than now, or if you are better off not gaming at all. You'll probably need to remove temptations from playing as best you can. Maybe you'll want to discontinue the services for your favorite games, or use my computer for your schoolwork because you are not used to playing games on mine. What do you think? How long do you think would be a good period to go without gaming? Pick a time you can reasonably go without gaming but one that is long enough to see if things get better when you are not wrapped up in it."

This example is one in which the parent and adult child work together on determining the duration of the gaming holiday.

Parents may also choose to impose the gaming holiday, especially for younger children. Parents may do this in the initial stages of addressing gaming problems, or they may do so after a trial period related to new gaming rules has been unsuccessful.

With younger children, the conversation around a gaming holiday may look like the following. Jennifer, the mother of a 12-year-old boy who plays Nintendo excessively, might say to him,

> *"Max, I know you enjoy playing Nintendo and other video games, and I realize that other kids your age also play these games. But I also think you've been playing them far too much lately, and it's time to take a break. It's time to focus on other activities like drawing, which you used to do a lot, or you could get involved again in soccer or another sport. For the next 4 weeks, we aren't going to do any gaming in the house—that includes you and your brother. I'm actually going to take the Nintendo away during this break period, so you'll want to think of some other things to do to fill your time. I found there is a new soccer league starting up next week on Tuesdays, and I will sign you up for that or help you with starting any new activity you want to try.*
>
> *"After 4 weeks, I will consider returning the Nintendo if you follow all the rules. The rules for the next 4 weeks are no gaming at all—that means no games on phones, iPads, computers, or anything else. Like I said, the Nintendo won't be here, nor will the games you play on the TV, so you won't be tempted by them. I know you need the computer for homework, but it will need to stay in the living room. It cannot be used for games, and if it is, the 4-week period will restart because I really want you to have a period without being distracted. Once you go a whole 4 weeks without gaming, I'll return the Nintendo, and we'll discuss reasonable limits for its use."*

If you do institute a gaming holiday, be sure to approach the decision definitively and assertively, but not aggressively, as in this example (see also Chapter 7). After the initial gaming holiday, Jennifer may settle upon rules about video game play with low limits such as no more than 12 hours a week, and no more than 2 hours per day (see Chapter 8). Her son may abide by these rules for a couple of months. One night, however, she may find her son playing late, after he was supposed to be in bed, and on a day he had already played for his allotted time. The discussion in response to a rule violation might go something like:

> *"Max, I am taking away the Nintendo. We discussed this a couple of months ago, and again earlier this week, when you didn't want to stop playing. Now you are up late on a school night, after you've already played for 2 hours this evening. I am locking the Nintendo in the trunk of my car now, and I will bring it to one of my friend's houses in the morning. I will consider bringing it back home if you do not play any games on the computer, the iPad, or your iPhone for the next 4 weeks. If you are playing these games here at home or if I hear of you playing them at school or friends' houses, I will ask my friend to give the Nintendo away. If you do go the next 4 weeks without playing video games, I will return it, but there are and will remain rules about when it can be used. If you break those rules again, I will take it away permanently."*

During the 4-week break from gaming, this mother would do best by no longer discussing the Nintendo. She can still replace the times Max usually plays games with alternate activities. She can reward any positive, nongaming behaviors, such as helping around the house. She can respond to her son assertively for any behaviors that are problematic.

When the 4 weeks are up, Jennifer should return the Nintendo as she had promised, presuming Max refrained from other forms of gaming during this period. The discussion might go like this:

> *"Max, I'm glad you went 4 weeks without gaming. I know it wasn't easy, and you weren't always happy about it. But I think you learned something important over this time. You discovered other things*

you like to do. Some I think you enjoyed even more than playing Nintendo. You seemed much happier to me when you came back from soccer games than you ever seemed after playing a video game. You also did more on the weekends with friends than you used to. You played soccer and went to the movies, to the mall, and to basketball games. Would you have done all that if the Nintendo were here the past 4 weeks? Overall, how did it feel going 4 weeks without playing?"

After the gaming holiday ends, even when it is parent imposed, it is important to encourage your child to think and talk about the period without gaming. What were the positive effects of not having the ability to play games? Were there some things he was glad happened because he was not gaming? What were the negative effects, if any? Does he feel like he will be able to control his gaming in the future? What could he do if he starts to feel like his gaming is getting out of control again?

If you and your child can answer these questions and respond to them honestly, you've come a long way in improving the situation. Make notes to remember the good things that came from a time away from gaming.

12

Moving forward and setting realistic long-term expectations

Sam's gaming remained at low levels throughout the remainder of the school year. He not only took up skiing but also joined the track team in the spring, along with a hiking club. He completed the school year with higher grades than he made the year before. Although he did not get all A's as his father would have liked, his grades definitely improved, and both he and his parents were proud of his achievements. His father almost forgot about his son's prior problems with gaming as the months went by. His mother reduced how often she monitored his gaming and quit locking up the Xbox controls because he rarely asked to play it, and when he did it was usually only for a half-hour. Sam was turning into a responsible teenager, and his parents were relieved.

Molly, on the other hand, benefited from a complete ban on gaming along with family therapy. Molly's mom decided to remove all gaming devices from the home and also discontinue home Internet service for 3 months. The first few weeks were really difficult, but eventually Molly got used to life without gaming when it was no longer a possibility at home. Although she initially refused her mother's offers of trying out new activities, Molly agreed to take a one-time trial class in karate, and she loved it. Although most of the other kids her age were in more advanced levels, the younger kids in the introductory level looked up to Molly, and it boosted her self-esteem. She was also good at it, and she rapidly advanced. Molly's mom signed her up for two karate classes a week, and also got back into the habit of playing old-fashioned board games with her daughter during their no-Internet period. She remembered how her daughter used to love Connect 4 and Battleship when she was younger. They pulled out these and other games and made one night a week a game night. After 3 months of no electronic gaming and gradually improving their relationship, Molly's mom thought it was time to rejoin the 21st century and bring the Internet back into their home. She was worried, however, about what this decision would mean for Molly's gaming.

By now you should have more confidence about what you as a parent can do to help your child overcome problems with gaming. The three R's are: Record, Replace, and Reward. Accurately recording and identifying game-playing patterns (Chapter 8) is an important skill that can help you better influence your child's gaming. Involving your child in new activities to replace gaming is another (Chapter 9). This can be a difficult goal to achieve, as it was in Molly's case, but when done successfully, gaming will no longer have the salience or value it once did. Rewarding nongaming behaviors (Chapter 10) is yet another strategy. Molly's mother finally was able to reward nongaming behaviors when gaming was no longer possible in the home. In conjunction with the three R's, communicating assertively (Chapter 7) is an ability related to all these skills and to good family functioning more generally. It underlies the successful implementation of all these steps. When reintroducing the Internet, Molly's mother would do best to use an assertive communication style regarding its use.

Learning to institute all these strategies is a process. Each step involves skills, and it will take time and practice to put them effectively into place. Learning new approaches to influence your child's behaviors is similar to learning a new language. No one begins to speak a new language in a day, or even in a week or a month. Similarly, you should not expect to master all these new skills rapidly. Molly's mother certainly needed time, and a long break from any gaming, to implement these strategies effectively.

As you begin to implement these steps, expect that it will take some time to change your child's behavior. Look for small steps in the right direction. Start to recognize when your new behaviors are having their intended effects on your child's behaviors, even in small ways. Forgive yourself when you make a mistake. No one is perfect, and especially not when trying something for the first time. Someone studying a new language has to practice saying words— often many times—to pronounce them correctly. You will need to try new methods—often multiple times—to get the result you desire. Likewise, your child needs to put new behaviors into practice for them to start to feel natural and to develop his or her own fluency with them. In Sam's case, his problems with gaming readily resolved. In Molly's, it took a complete ban on gaming and months of time and effort to make an inroad.

This last chapter is a guide toward setting reasonable expectations for both yourself and your child. You should expect some setbacks, as well as some miscommunications along the way. Even after progress is made, there may be some regressions toward old behavior patterns, for both you and your child. Lapses back to gaming on the part of your child, or toward passive or aggressive responding on your part, do not signify failure. On the contrary, if you recognize the reemergence of old patterns, they can serve as important learning opportunities. Ultimately, developing new behaviors can promote long-term success for both you and your child.

Reasonable expectations for your child

According to available research, between 14% and 65% of adolescents with gaming problems resolve their difficulties within 1 to 2 years.[1] As you integrate the changes this book outlines, your child should experience improvements within a few months, rather than years. How long it takes will depend, in part, on your ability to make the home environment and your own behaviors less conducive toward gaming and more supportive of other activities.

Developing positive recreational activities is critical for any balanced lifestyle. It will take time for your child to find other ways to spend free time and to relax. Hobbies are not acquired overnight. Give your child sufficient time to try multiple new things before expecting her to find something she enjoys. It will take time before new interests compete with gaming. Every little step in the direction of acquiring new and healthier ways to spend free time is progress.

As your child tries out new activities and reduces or stops his gaming, be sure to recognize that these changes may not be permanent. A change can trigger old behavior patterns, just as it can signal new ones. For example, your child may have taken a part-time job over the summer and started playing tennis regularly. During the vacation period, gaming may have been intermittent and nonproblematic. Once school begins, he may have *more* free time than he did in the summer. Coming home from school may automatically signal turning on a game. Therefore, it is critical that monitoring gaming occurs long term, and that you regularly discuss goals with respect to gaming, both your child's and your own. Encourage frank and open discussions about gaming and help your child to address potential concerns as they are emerging.

Expect some lapses, especially during stressful or transition periods. A *lapse* is a temporary resumption in the problem behavior. It may relate to one gaming episode, or a week or more of excessive playing. What distinguishes a lapse from a *relapse* is the extent and duration of problems that arise. If your child lapses, this does not necessarily mean that significant problems will resume. It will not be as difficult as it was initially to reinstate the earlier gaming goals if you, and your child, quickly recognize the lapse. Lapses can be important learning experiences. If your child lapses and expresses concern or regret, this represents a very positive event. Learning to recognize when one's behaviors are moving in a wrong direction is an important step to growth and long-term change. Discussing what happened and why, and brainstorming other methods for handling similar situations in the future without gaming, can prevent problems from progressing. This process should lead to self-discovery, not shame.

Let's return to the case of Pete, Amy, and Sam. One day, Amy came home from work to find Sam entrenched in a game on the Xbox. She asked him how long he'd been playing and she knew he was lying when he said he'd just turned it on. She asked him to turn it off, and he said he would in a minute, right after he finished this game. Minutes turned into an hour, and he still hadn't stopped playing. When Amy confronted her son the third time, he started yelling at her that it was summer, and all the other kids got to play as much as they wanted. He'd already cleaned up the yard that day like she had asked and she had no right to try to control what he did with his free time.

Amy could feel her old reactions to Sam's gaming bubbling to the surface. In the past, she would have just walked away, and let him keep on gaming. She remembered the gaming contract. Although the last one they had signed "expired" months ago, she decided to pull it out. She brought it to Sam while he was playing and said,

> *"Sam, I know how hard you've worked to keep your gaming at bay over the past many months. You've made such progress, and I've been so proud of you. Neither of us want this to go back to the way it was earlier. Please turn off the game right now, and let's talk about what happened."*

Amy used the Communication Tips from Chapter 7 to address the issue promptly with her son. Once Sam ceased the game, he was able to talk about it. He said he had missed playing and once he started, he got really involved in an exciting part and just didn't want to stop until it was over. He lost track of time while he was playing. He also realized that if he played without a timer on, it was just too easy to forget how long he had been playing. He had been home alone the whole day, with few activities planned, and there had been no external controls on his gaming.

As children get older, they will have more responsibilities, as well as more freedom. New responsibilities and roles can promote natural changes. Growing older, staying home alone, graduating, getting a new job, or changing schools can alter old behavior patterns and assist in breaking old habits as well as promoting new ones. If you can help your child overcome his problems with gaming now, it is likely he will remember those successes later. If your child experiences difficulties with gaming (or another addictive behavior) years down the road, he may recall how he resolved them previously. Your child may even ask you for assistance!

Reasonable expectations for yourself

I hope you have learned from this book that you can help your child change his or her behavior in part by changing your own. In reviewing the chapters, your concerns about your child's gaming behaviors may have decreased. You may have discovered that gaming problems can become much more severe than your child has experienced. If this is the case, then you can still utilize these steps in a preventive manner. By closely recording gaming, you can objectively assess whether it is increasing over time or if it is beginning to lead to problems at some point. By rearranging the environment to better uncover gaming and by minimizing access to gaming devices in private areas (e.g., bedrooms), you can likely prevent more significant problems from arising in the future. If your child participates in other recreational activities, you can encourage them actively, especially during times you are worried about gaming intensifying or other problems emerging. In addition, communicating effectively with your child can be a two-way street. As your child experiences you reacting more assertively and less aggressively or passively, you may begin to see your child's communication styles mirror your positive one.

Some parents reading this book already know that their child has a severe problem with gaming. If you are one such parent, it is critical to understand that there may be little you can do to stop the gaming behaviors short of removing all gaming devices (see Chapter 11). Stopping the play abruptly, however, will not resolve the underlying issues. Any school or interpersonal problems that arose from the playing or precipitated it will not be solved. Therefore, it is imperative that you as a parent take steps beyond just removing gaming devices from the home. Encouraging participation in other recreational activities is key, as is developing more effective communication styles. Accessing professional mental health care for other problems may be needed. Molly's example is a case in point. Molly's mom needed professional advice to assure her that removal of the Internet and all gaming was necessary. Once gaming was no longer interfering with the development of other hobbies and pastimes, it became easier to integrate Molly in new activities. Although it took weeks, her anger eventually dissipated, and both mother and daughter could begin to communicate more effectively.

Whether your child has minimal or severe difficulties with video game playing, it is important to recognize that your behaviors influence your child, no matter his age. Just as your child might lapse or relapse to gaming at some point in the future, you too might return to previous behavior or communication patterns. It will be important to be diligent in monitoring and addressing your own behaviors over time, as well as those of your child.

Once gaming stops or becomes minimal, you certainly don't need to continue tracking it several times a day as Chapter 8 describes. However, a quick consideration of the amount of time your child is playing on a weekly basis can be informative. If your child is playing regularly, it might be best to still monitor gaming daily to ensure that goals or limits are not exceeded. If the playing is less regular and clearly under a few hours per week, weekly monitoring may be sufficient. If you consider the frequency and duration of your child's gaming at least weekly, you will be in a good position to recognize quickly if it begins to increase. Discussions with your child or more overt methods to prevent initiation of gaming episodes during high-risk times (Replacing and Rewarding, Chapters 9 and 10) may be in order.

Importantly, you will have good knowledge of what successfully stopped excessive playing in the past. Implementing similar or parallel strategies preventively should help reduce difficulties moving forward. If your older or adult child has fallen into a full-blown relapse and is gaming as much as or more than he did previously, you may need to allow the natural consequences of excessive play to occur (Chapter 7). In this manner, your child will have to accept responsibility for his behaviors. Alternatively, you may need to stop enabling gaming in any way and remove all gaming possibilities from the home. In Molly's case, any new contract allowing even minimal gaming would need to specify clear and immediate consequences of breaking the rules, which may include another discontinuation of Internet service.

You should assess not only your child's gaming at least weekly over the course of the next several months and years, but also his or her other extracurricular activities. Monitor what your child is doing, and with whom he or she is doing it, at least weekly. If there are no recreational activities in a week, or fewer than usual for several weeks in a row, you may want to become more involved. Unoccupied free time is a major risk factor for development of gaming problems as well as other difficulties. If your child stops participating in a previously enjoyed activity, he or she may be at risk for resuming gaming. School vacations, a change in sports seasons, or an alteration of social groups may be reason to more carefully consider what your child is doing with free time and to proactively fill that extra time with other activities. You can always refer back to the list of recreational activities and steps in Chapter 9 to assist your child in becoming involved with new activities as she or he matures.

Similarly, set aside time to consider your own behaviors with respect to rewarding your child, and rewarding yourself. If problems with gaming resolve, you will no longer be rewarding your child regularly for not playing. You can reward your child for other behaviors, and rewards can come in many varieties. All kids would like to hear a positive statement from their parent at least once a week, if not daily. Consider each night before you go to bed whether you rewarded your child at least once verbally that day. If you go a few days in a row without doing so, try to congratulate or appreciate your child for something he or she did as soon as possible. You should reward your child for the next small step she takes in a positive direction, even if it involves something as simple as taking a dish to the sink after dinner or bringing in the mail. Whether your child is still in elementary school or is now an adult, remember to reward her for all she is doing well!

Good communication skills are not easy to develop, and they require effort to maintain, especially when days get busy and people get stressed. Rewarding your child for positive behaviors is one small step toward better communication. Also try to set aside a little time each week to consider instances in which you responded assertively, passively, and aggressively. Reward yourself for assertive communications each day, whether they are in relation to your interactions with your child, your partner, another family member, or a coworker. If it becomes all too easy to identify passive or aggressive responses but difficult to name assertive ones, it is time to reconsider more actively your own communication style.

The short- and long-term effectiveness of all these strategies will depend in part on how ready you are to change. By completing the exercises in this book, you will be in a better position to positively impact not only your own behavior, but that of your child and others around you as well. Change is never easy, and the path of least resistance is of course always the easiest to follow. If you are reading this book, you have taken the first step in altering your own behavior. That effort sets the stage for assisting your child in changing his or her gaming behaviors. It may even be the most important step you take in improving your lifelong relationship with your child.

Notes

Preface

1. American Medical Association, 2007.

Chapter 1

1. Spragg, 2015.
2. Lenhart, Kahne, Middaugh, et al., 2008.
3. Gentile, 2009a.
4. Chuang, 2006.
5. Salmon, 2010.

Chapter 2

1. Király, Griffiths, Urbán, et al., 2014; Ko, Yen, Yen, Lin, and Yang, 2007; Li, Zhang, Lu, Zhang, and Wang, 2014; van Rooij, Schoenmakers, van de Eijnden, and van de Mheen, 2010.
2. US Census, 2013.
3. Internet World Stats, 2014.
4. Nielsen Report, 2011.
5. Gentile, 2009a.
6. Gentile, 2009a.
7. Cummings and Vandewater, 2007.

8. Ko, Yen, Chen, Chen, and Yen, 2005; Salguero and Morán, 2002; Thomas and Martin, 2010.

9. https://www.twitch.tv/directory/game/Street%20Fighter%20V

10. http://www.espn.com/esports/story/_/id/18202274/capcom-cup-2016-world-champion-du-nuckledu-dang-get-check-[moms]-not-going-believe-me

11. http://www.thescoreesports.com/streetfighter/news/12063-capcom-cup-hits-87-000-viewers-on-espn-2)

12. Brunborg, Mentzoni, and Melkevik, 2013; Choo, Gentile, Sim, Li, Khoo, and Liau, 2010; Desai, Krishnan-Sarin, Cavallo, and Potenza, 2010; Festl, Scharkow, and Quandt, 2013; Gentile, 2009a; Haagsma, Pieterse, and Peters, 2012; Johansson and Götestam, 2004; King, Delfabbro, Zwaans, and Kaptsis, 2013; Lemmens, Valkenberg, and Peter, 2009; Lemmens, Vlkenberg, and Gentile, 2015; Mentzoni, Brunborg, and Molde, 2011; Müller, Janikian, and Dreier, 2015; Papáy, Urbán, and Griffiths, 2013; Rehbein, Kleimann, and Mössle, 2010; Rehbein, Kliem, Baier, Mössle, and Petry, 2015; Salguero and Morán, 2002; Thomas and Martin, 2010; van Rooij, Schoenmakers, Vermulst, van den Eijnden, and van de Mheen, 2011; Wittek, Finseras, Pallesen, et al., 2015.

13. Haagsma, 2012; King, Delfabbro, Zwaans, and Kaptsis, 2013; Müller, Janikian, and Dreier, 2015; Rehbein, Kleimann, and Mössle, 2010; Rehbein, Kliem, Baier, Mössle, and Petry, 2015; van Rooij, Schoenmakers, Vermulst, van den Eijnden, and van de Mheen, 2011; Wittek, Finseras, Pallesen, et al., 2015.

14. Choo, Gentile, Sim, Li, Khoo, and Liau, 2010; Gentile, 2009a; Salguero and Morán, 2002.

15. Gentile, 2009a.

16. Gentile, Choo, Liau, et al., 2011; Scharkow, Festle, and Quandt, 2014; van Rooij, Schoenmakers, Vermulst, van den Eijnden, and van de Mheen, 2011.

Chapter 3

1. American Psychiatric Association, 2013.

2. Petry, Rehbein, Gentile, et al., 2014.

3. Choo, Gentile, Sim, Li, Khoo, and Liau, 2010; Gentile, 2009a; Haagsma, Pieterse, and Peters, 2012; Johansson and Götestam, 2004; Rehbein, Kliem, Baier, Mössle, and Petry, 2015.

4. Festl, Scharkow, and Quandt, 2013; Gentile, 2009a; Haagsma, Pieterse, and Peters, 2012; Johansson and Götestam, 2004; Lemmens, Valkenburg, and

Gentile, 2015; Rehbein, Kleimann, and Mössle, 2010; Rehbein, Kliem, Baier, Mössle, and Petry, 2015; but see Choo, Gentile, Sim, Li, Khoo, and Liau, 2010.

5. Rehbein, Kliem, Baier, Mössle, and Petry, 2015.

6. Choo, Gentile, Sim, Li, Khoo, and Liau, 2010; Gentile, 2009a; Rehbein, Kliem, Baier, Mössle, and Petry, 2015.

7. Rehbein, Kliem, Baier, Mössle, and Petry, 2015.

8. Keyes, Krueger, Grant, and Hasin, 2011.

9. Choo, Gentile, Sim, Li, Khoo, and Liau, 2010; Festl, Scharkow, and Quandt, 2013; Gentile, 2009a; Haagsma, Pieterse, and Peters, 2012; Rehbein, Kliem, Baier, Mössle, and Petry, 2015.

10. Rehbein, Kleimann, and Mössle, 2010.

11. Rehbein, Kliem, Baier, Mössle, and Petry, 2015.

12. Porter, Starcevic, Berle, and Fenech, 2010.

13. Gentile, 2009a.

14. Festl, Scharkow, and Quandt, 2013.

15. Rehbein, Kliem, Baier, Mössle, and Petry, 2015.

16. Choo, Gentile, Sim, Li, Khoo, and Liau, 2010; Gentile, 2009a; Johansson and Götestam, 2004; Lemmens, Valkenburg, and Gentile, 2015; Rehbein, Kliem, Baier, Mössle, and Petry, 2015; Salguero and Morán, 2002.

17. Choo, Gentile, Sim, Li, Khoo, and Liau, 2010; Festl, Scharkow, and Quandt, 2013; Gentile, 2009a; Haagsma, Pieterse, and Peters, 2012; Johansson and Götestam, 2004; Rehbein, Kliem, Baier, Mössle, and Petry, 2015; Salguero and Morán, 2002.

18. Blanco, Hasin, Petry, Stinson, and Grant, 2006; Strong and Kahler, 2007.

19. Johansson and Götestam, 2004; Lemmens, Valkenburg, and Gentile, 2015; Rehbein, Kliem, Baier, Mössle, and Petry, 2015.

Chapter 4

1. Baer, Saran, and Green, 2012; Johansson and Götestam, 2004; Lemmens, Valkenburg, and Gentile, 2015; Rehbein, Kliem, Baier, Mössle, and Petry, 2015.

2. Gentile, 2009a.

3. Haagsma, Pieterse, and Peters, 2012; Mentzoni, Brunborg, and Molde, 2011; Rehbein, Kleimann, and Mössle, 2010; van Rooij, Schoenmakers, van den Eijnden, and van de Mheen, 2010.

4. Rehbein, Kleimann, and Mössle, 2010.

5. Longman, O'Connor, and Obst, 2009.

6. Rehbein, Kleimann, and Mössle, 2010.

7. Smyth, 2007.

8. Mentzoni, Brunborg, and Molde, 2011.

9. Desai, Krishnan-Sarin, Cavallo, and Potenza, 2010; Gentile, 2009a; Mentzoni, Brunborg, and Molde, 2011; Müller, Janikian, and Dreier, 2015.

10. Rehbein, Kleimann, and Mössle, 2010.

11. Haagsma, Pieterse, and Peters, 2012; Mentzoni, Brunborg, Molde, et al., 2011

12. Festl, Scharkow, and Quandt, 2013; Haagsma, Pieterse, and Peters, 2012; Mentzoni, Brunborg, Molde, et al., 2011; Wittek, Finseras, Pallesen, et al., 2015.

13. Desai, Krishnan-Sarin, Cavallo, and Potenza, 2010; Gentile, 2009a.

14. Desai, Krishnan-Sarin, Cavallo, and Potenza, 2010.

15. Wittek, Finseras, Pallesen, et al., 2015.

16. Desai, 2010; Mentzoni, Brunborg, and Molde, 2011; van Rooij, Schoenmakers, Vermulst, van den Eijnden, and van de Mheen, 2011.

17. Romer, Bagdasarov, and More, 2013.

18. Han and Renshaw, 2012.

19. Gentile, Choo, Liau, et al., 2011; Lo, Wang, and Fang, 2005.

20. Yee, 2006.

21. Choo, Gentile, Sim, Li, Khoo, and Liau, 2010; Rehbein, Kleimann, and Mössle, 2010.

22. Bioulac, Arfi, and Bouvard, 2008; Chan and Rabinowitz, 2006; Gentile, 2009a.

23. Swing, Gentile, Anderson, and Walsh, 2010.

24. Han, Lee, Na, et al., 2009.

25. van Rooij, Kuss, Griffiths, et al., 2014, Porter, Starcevic, Berle, and Fenech, 2010, Desai, Krishnan-Sarin, Cavallo, and Potenza, 2010, Walther, Morgenstern, and Hanewinkel, 2012.

26. E.g., Ko, Liu, Hsiao, et al., 2009; Ko, Liu, Yen, Chen, and Lin, 2013; Sun, Ying, Seetohul, et al., 2012.

27. Anthony and Petronis, 1995

28. Anderson, Shibuya, Ihori, et al., 2010; Calvert, 2017.

29. Anderson, Sakamoto, Gentile, et al., 2008.

30. Ferguson, 2007; Ferguson, Rueda, Cruz, Ferguson, Fritz, and Smith, 2008.

31. Brown, Harris *v.* Entertainment Merchants Association, 2011.

Chapter 5

1. Piaget, 1962.

2. Granic, Lobel, and Engels, 2014.

3. Gentile, Anderson, Yukawa, et al., 2009b.

4. Gentile, Anderson, Yukawa, et al., 2009b.

5. Przybylski, 2014.

6. Romer, Bagdasarov, and More, 2013.

7. LeBlanc, Chaput, McFarlane, et al., 2013.

8. Simons, Bernaards, and Slinger, 2012.

9. Plow and Finlayson, 2011.

10. Carlson, Fulton, Lee, Foley, and Heitzler, 2010; Romer, Bagdasarov, and More, 2013.

11. Dye, Green, and Bavelier, 2009.

12. Bavelier, Achtman, Mani, and Föcker, 2012.

13. Bariqued, Kranz, Voss, et al., 2014.

14. Anguera, Boccanfuso, Rintoul, et al., 2013.

15. Jalink, Goris, Heineman, Pierie, and ten Cate Hoedemaker, 2014.

16. Jackson, Witt, Games, Fitzgerald, von Eye, and Zhao, 2012.

17. Cooper, Khatib, Treuille, et al., 2010.

Chapter 6

1. Gentile, 2009a.

2. Petry, Rehbein, Gentile, et al., 2014.

3. Cohen, Feinn, Arias, and Kranzler, 2007.

4. Hodgins and el-Guebaly, 2000.

5. Cohen, Feinn, Arias, and Kranzler, 2007; Petry, 2005; Slutske, 2006.

6. Gentile, Choo, Liau, et al., 2011; Scharkow, Festle, and Quandt, 2014; van Rooij, Schoenmakers, Vermulst, van den Eijnden, and van de Mheen, 2011.

7. Lee, Chassin, and Villalta, 2013.

8. Shaffer, Hall, and Vander Bilt, 1999.

9. Slutske, Jackson, and Sher, 2003.

10. King, Delfabbro, Griffiths, and Gradisar, 2011; King and Delfabbro, 2014; Petry, Rehbein, Ko, and O'Brien, 2015b; Winkler, Dörsing, Rief, Shen, and Glombiewski, 2013; Zajac, Ginley, Chang, and Petry, 2017.

11. Cuijpers, Andersson, Donker, and van Straten, 2011; Miller and Wilbourne, 2002.

12. Young, 2007.

13. Monti, Kadden, Rohsenow, Cooney, and Abrams, 2002.

14. Cash, Rae, Steel, and Winkler, 2012.

Chapter 7

1. Adapted from Miller and Heather, 1998; Monti, Kadden, Rohsenow, Cooney, and Abrams, 2002.

Chapter 8

1. Dishion and McMahon, 1998.

2. Gentile, Reimer, Nathanson, Walsh, and Eisenmann, 2014.

3. Roberts and Foehr, 2008; Smith, Gradisar, and King, 2015.

4. Olson, Kutner, and Warner, 2007.

5. Gentile, 2009a.

6. Carlson, Fulton, Lee, Foley, and Heitzler, 2010.

7. Rideout, 2010.

8. Council on Communications and Media, 2013.

9. American Academy of Pediatrics, 2016.

10. Council on Communications and Media, 2013.

Chapter 9

1. Adapted from Monti, Kadden, Rohsenow, Cooney, and Abrams, 2002.

Chapter 10

1. Dutra, Stathpoulou, Basden, Leyro, Powers, and Otto, 2008.
2. Krishnan-Sarin, Cavallo, and Cooney, 2013; Stanger, Ryan, Scherer, Norton, and Budney, 2015.
3. Lussier, Heil, Mongeon, Badger, and Higgins, 2006.
4. Petry, Alessi, and Rash, 2013a.
5. Volpp, John, Troxel, Norton, Fassbender, and Loewenstein, 2008; Petry, Barry, and Pescatello, 2011.
6. Petry, Andrade, Barry, and Byrne, 2013b.
7. Petry, Alessi, and Byrne, 2015a.
8. Hunt and Azrin, 1973; Meyers, Roozen, and Smith, 2011; Roozen, Boulogne, van Tulder, van den Brink, De Jong, and Kerkhof, 2004.
9. Ferster and Skinner, 1957.

Chapter 12

1. Gentile, Choo, Liau, et al., 2011; Scharkow, Festle, and Quandt, 2014; van Rooij, Schoenmakers, Vermulst, van den Eijnden, and van de Mheen, 2011.

References

Achab S, Nicolier M, Mauny F, Monnin J, Trojak B, Vandel P, Sechter D, Gorwood P, Haffen E. Massively multiplayer online role-playing games: comparing characteristics of addict vs non-addict online recruited gamers in a French adult population. *BMC Psychiatry.* 2011;26(11):144.

American Academy of Pediatrics, Council on Communications and Media. Media use in school-aged children and adolescents. *Pediatrics.* 2016;138(5):e20162592.

American Medical Association. Report of the Council on Science and Public Health. 2007. Available at: http://psychcentral.com/blog/images/ csaph12a07.pdf

American Psychiatric Association. *Diagnostic and Statistical Manual of Mental Disorders.* 5th ed. Washington, DC: American Psychiatric Association Press.

Anderson CA, Sakamoto A, Gentile DA, Ihori N, Shibuya A, Yukawa S, Naito M, Kobayashi K. Longitudinal effects of violent video games on aggression in Japan and the United States. *Pediatrics.* 2008;122(5):e1067–1072.

Anderson CA, Shibuya A, Ihori N, Swing EL, Bushman BJ, Sakamoto A, Rothstein HR, Saleem M. Violent video game effects on aggression, empathy, and prosocial behavior in Eastern and Western countries: a meta-analytic review. *Psychol Bull.* 2010;136(2):151–173.

Anguera JA, Boccanfuso J, Rintoul JL, Al-Hashimi O, Faraji F, Janowich J, Kong E, Larraburo Y, Rolle C, Johnston E, Gazzaley A. Video game training enhances cognitive control in older adults. *Nature.* 2013;501(7465):97–101.

Anthony JC, Petronis KR. Early-onset drug use and risk of later drug problems. *Drug Alcohol Depend.* 1995;40:9–15.

Baer S, Saran K, Green DA. Computer/gaming station use in youth: correlations among use, addiction and functional impairment. *Paediatr Child Health.* 2012;17(8):427–431.

Baniqued PL, Kranz MB, Voss MW, Lee H, Cosman JD, Severson J, Kramer AF. Cognitive training with casual video games: points to consider. *Front Psychol.* 2014;4:1010.

Bavelier D, Achtman RL, Mani M, Föcker J. Neural bases of selective attention in action video game players. *Vision Res.* 2012;61:132–143.

Bioulac S, Arfi L, Bouvard MP. Attention deficit/hyperactivity disorder and video games: a comparative study of hyperactive and control children. *Eur Psychiatry.* 2008;23(2):134–141.

Blanco C, Hasin DS, Petry N, Stinson FS, Grant BF. Sex differences in subclinical and DSM-IV pathological gambling: results from the National Epidemiologic Survey on Alcohol and Related Conditions. *Psychol Med.* 2006;36(7):943–953.

Calvert SL, Appelbaum M, Dodge KA, Graham S, Nagayama Hall GC, Hamby S, Fasig-Caldwell LG, Citkowicz M, Galloway DP, Hedges LV. The American Psychological Association Task Force assessment of violent video games: science in the service of public interest. *Am Psychol.* 2017;72(2):126–143.

Carlson SA, Fulton JE, Lee SM, Foley JT, Heitzler C, Huhman M. Influence of limit-setting and participation in physical activity on youth screen time. *Pediatrics.* 2010;126(1):e89–96.

Cash H, Rae CD, Steel AH, Winkler A. Internet addiction: a brief summary of research and practice. *Curr Psychiatry Rev.* 2012;8(4):292–298.

Chan PA, Rabinowitz T. A cross-sectional analysis of video games and attention deficit hyperactivity disorder symptoms in adolescents. *Ann Gen Psychiatry.* 2006;24(5):16.

Choo H, Gentile DA, Sim T, Li D, Khoo A, Liau AK. Pathological video-gaming among Singaporean youth. *Ann Acad Med Singapore.* 2010;39(11):822–829.

Chuang YC. Massively multiplayer online role-playing game-induced seizures: a neglected health problem in Internet addiction. *Cyberpsychol Behav.* 2006;9:451–456.

Cohen E, Feinn R, Arias A, Kranzler HR. Alcohol treatment utilization: findings from the National Epidemiologic Survey on Alcohol and Related Conditions. *Drug Alcohol Depend.* 2007;86(2–3):214–221.

Cooper S, Khatib F, Treuille A, Barbero J, Lee J, Beenen M, Popović Z. Predicting protein structures with a multiplayer online game. *Nature.* 2010;466:756–760.

Council on Communications and Media. Policy statement: children, adolescents, and the media. *Pediatrics.* 2013;132(5): 958–961.

Cuijpers P, Andersson G, Donker T, van Straten A. Psychological treatment of depression: results of a series of meta-analyses. *Nord J Psychiatry.* 2011;65(6):354–364.

Cummings HM, Vandewater EA. Relation of adolescent video game play to time spent in other activities. *Arch Pediatr Adolesc Med.* 2007;161(7):684–689.

Desai RA, Krishnan-Sarin S, Cavallo D, Potenza MN. Video-gaming among high school students: health correlates, gender differences, and problematic gaming. *Pediatrics.* 2010;126(6):e1414–1424.

Dishion TJ, McMahon RJ. Parental monitoring and the prevention of child and adolescent problem behavior: a conceptual and empirical formulation. *Clin Child Fam Psychol Rev.* 1998;1(1):61–75.

Durkee T, Kaess M, Carli V, Parzer P, Wasserman C, Floderus B, Apter A, Balazs J, Barzilay S, Bobes J, Brunner R, Corcoran P, Cosman D, Cotter P, Despalins R, Graber N, Guillemin F, Haring C, Kahn JP, Mandelli L, Marusic D, Mészáros G, Musa GJ, Postuvan V, Resch F, Saiz PA, Sisask M, Varnik A, Sarchiapone M, Hoven CW, Wasserman D. Prevalence of pathological internet use among adolescents in Europe: demographic and social factors. *Addiction.* 2012;107(12):2210–2222.

Dutra L, Stathopoulou G, Basden SL, Leyro TM, Powers MB, Otto MW. A meta-analytic review of psychosocial interventions for substance use disorders. *Am J Psychiatry.* 2008;165(2):179–187.

Dye MWG, Green CS, Bavelier D. Increasing speed of processing with action video games. *Curr Dir Psychol Sci.* 2009;18(6): 321–326.

Ferguson CJ. The good, the bad and the ugly: a meta-analytic review of positive and negative effects of violent video games. *Psychiatr Q.* 2007;78(4):309–316.

Ferguson CJ, Rueda SM, Cruz AM, Ferguson DE, Fritz S, Smith SM. Violent video games and aggression: causal relationship or byproduct of family violence and intrinsic violence motivation? *Crim Just Behav.* 2008;35:311–332.

Ferster CB, Skinner BF. *Schedules of Reinforcement.* New York, NY: Appleton-Century Crofts; 1957.

Festl R, Scharkow M, Quandt T. Problematic computer game use among adolescents, younger and older adults. *Addiction.* 2013;108(3):592–599.

Gentile DA. Pathological video-game use among youth ages 8 to 18: a national study. *Psychol Sci.* 2009a;20:594–602.

Gentile DA, Anderson CA, Yukawa S, Ihori N, Saleem M, Ming LK, Shibuya A, Liau AK, Khoo A, Bushman BJ, Rowell Huesmann L, Sakamoto A. The effects of prosocial video games on prosocial behaviors: international evidence from correlational, longitudinal, and experimental studies. *Pers Soc Psychol Bull.* 2009b;35(6):752–763.

Gentile DA, Choo H, Liau A, Sim T, Li D, Fung D, Khoo A. Pathological video game use among youths: a two-year longitudinal study. *Pediatrics.* 2011;127(2):e319–329.

Gentile DA, Reimer RA, Nathanson AI, Walsh DA, Eisenmann JC. Protective effects of parental monitoring of children's media use: a prospective study. *JAMA Pediatr.* 2014;168(5):479–484.

Granic I, Lobel A, Engels RC. The benefits of playing video games. *Am Psychol.* 2014;69:66–78.

Haagsma MC, Pieterse ME, Peters O. The prevalence of problematic video gamers in the Netherlands. *Cyberpsychol Behav Soc Netw.* 2012;15(3):162–168.

Han DH, Lee YS, Na C, Ahn JY, Chung US, Daniels MA, Haws CA, Renshaw PF. The effect of methylphenidate on Internet video game play in children with attention-deficit/hyperactivity disorder. *Compr Psychiatry.* 2009;50:251–256.

Han DH, Renshaw PF. Bupropion in the treatment of problematic online game play in patients with major depressive disorder. *J Psychopharmacol.* 2012;26(5):689–696.

Henggeler SW, Chapman JE, Rowland MD, Halliday-Boykins CA, Randall J, Shackelford J, Schoenwald SK. Statewide adoption and initial implementation of contingency management for substance-abusing adolescents. *J Consult Clin Psychol.* 2008;76(4):556–567.

Hodgins DC, el-Guebaly N. Natural and treatment-assisted recovery from gambling problems: a comparison of resolved and active gamblers. *Addiction.* 2000;95(5):777–789.

Hunt GM, Azrin NH. A community-reinforcement approach to alcoholism. *Behav Res Ther.* 1973;11:91–104.

Internet World Stats. 2014; http://www.internetworldstats.com/stats9.htm.

Jackson LA, Witt EA, Games AI, Fitzgerald HE, von Eye A, Zhao Y. Information technology use and creativity: findings from the Children and Technology Project. *Computers Human Behav.* 2012; 28:370–376.

Jalink MB, Goris J, Heineman E, Pierie JP, ten Cate Hoedemaker HO. The effects of video games on laparoscopic simulator skills. *Am J Surg.* 2014;208(1):151–156.

Johansson A, Götestam KG. Problems with computer games without monetary reward: similarity to pathological gambling. *Psychol Rep.* 2004;95:641–650.

Keyes KM, Krueger RF, Grant BF, Hasin DS. Alcohol craving and the dimensionality of alcohol disorders. *Psychol Med.* 2011;41(3):629–640.

King DL, Delfabbro PH. Internet gaming disorder treatment: a review of definitions of diagnosis and treatment outcome. *J Clin Psychol.* 2014;70(10):942–955.

King DL, Delfabbro PH, Griffiths MD, Gradisar M. Assessing clinical trials of Internet addiction treatment: a systematic review and CONSORT evaluation. *Clin Psychol Rev.* 2011;31(7):1110–1116.

King DL Delfabbro PH, Zwaans T, Kaptsis D. Clinical features and axis I comorbidity of Australian adolescent pathological Internet and video game users. *Aust N Z J Psychiatry.* 2013;47(11):1058–1067.

Király O, Griffiths MD, Urbán R, Farkas J, Kökönyei G, Elekes Z, Tamás D, Demetrovics Z. Problematic Internet use and problematic online gaming are not the same: findings from a large nationally representative adolescent sample. *Cyberpsychol Behav Soc Netw.* 2014;17(12):749–754.

Ko CH, Liu GC, Hsiao S, Yen JY, Yang MJ, Lin WC, Yen CF, Chen CS. Brain activities associated with gaming urge of online gaming addiction. *J Psychiatr Res.* 2009;43(7):739–747.

Ko CH, Liu GC, Yen JY, Yen CF, Chen CS, Lin WC. The brain activations for both cue-induced gaming urge and smoking craving among subjects comorbid with Internet gaming addiction and nicotine dependence. *J Psychiatr Res.* 2013;47(4):486–493.

Ko CH, Yen JY, Chen CC, Chen SH, Yen CF. Gender differences and related factors affecting online gaming addiction among Taiwanese adolescents. *J Nerv Ment Dis.* 2005;193(4):273–277.

Ko CH, Yen JY, Yen CF, Lin HC, Yang MJ. Factors predictive for incidence and remission of internet addiction in young adolescents: a prospective study. *Cyberpsychol Behav.* 2007;10(4):545–551.

Krishnan-Sarin S, Cavallo DA, Cooney JL, Schepis TS, Kong G, Liss TB, Liss AK, McMahon TJ, Nich C, Babuscio T, Rounsaville BJ, Carroll KM. An exploratory randomized controlled trial of a novel high-school-based smoking cessation intervention for adolescent smokers using abstinence-contingent incentives and cognitive behavioral therapy. *Drug Alcohol Depend.* 2013; 132:346–351.

LeBlanc AG, Chaput JP, McFarlane A, Colley RC, Thivel D, Biddle SJ, Maddison R, Leatherdale ST, Tremblay MS. Active video games and health indicators in children and youth: a systematic review. *PLoS One.* 2013;8(6):e65351.

Lee MR, Chassin L, Villalta IK. Maturing out of alcohol involvement: transitions in latent drinking statuses from late adolescence to adulthood. *Dev Psychopathol.* 2013;25:1137–1153.

Lemmens JS, Valkenburg PM, Gentile DA. The Internet Gaming Disorder Scale. *Psychol Assess*. 2015;27(2):567–582.

Lemmens JS, Valkenburg P, Peter J. Development and validation of a game addiction scale for adolescents. *Media Psychology*. 2009;12:77–95.

Lenhart A, Kahne J, Middaugh E, Macgill A, Evans C, Vitak J. Teens, video games, and civics: teens' gaming experiences are diverse and include significant social interaction and civic engagement. *Pew Internet & American Life Project*. 2008. http://www.pewinternet.org/Reports/2008/Teens-Video-Games-and-Civics.aspx.

Li Y, Zhang X, Lu F, Zhang Q, Wang Y. Internet addiction among elementary and middle school students in China: a nationally representative sample study. *Cyberpsychol Behav Soc Netw*. 2014;17(2):111–116.

Lo SK, Wang CC, Fang W. Physical interpersonal relationships and social anxiety among online game players. *Cyberpsychol Behav*. 2005;8(1):15–20.

Longman H, O'Connor E, Obst P. The effect of social support derived from World of Warcraft on negative psychological symptoms. *Cyberpsychol Behav*. 2009;12(5):563–566.

Lussier JP, Heil SH, Mongeon JA, Badger GJ, Higgins ST. A meta-analysis of voucher-based reinforcement therapy for substance use disorders. *Addiction*. 2006;101(2):192–203.

Mentzoni RA, Brunborg GS, Molde H, Myrseth H, Skouverøe KJ, Hetland J, Pallesen S. Problematic video game use: estimated prevalence and associations with mental and physical health. *Cyberpsychol Behav Soc Netw*. 2011;14(10):591–596.

Meyers RJ, Roozen HG, Smith JE. The community reinforcement approach: an update of the evidence. *Alcohol Res Health*. 2011;33(4):380–388.

Miller WR, Heather N. *Treating Addictive Behaviors*. 2nd ed. New York, NY: Plenum Press; 1998.

Miller WR, Wilbourne PL. Mesa Grande: a methodological analysis of clinical trials of treatments for alcohol use disorders. *Addiction*. 2002;97:265–277.

Monti P, Kadden R, Rohsenow, D, Cooney N, Abrams D. *Treating Alcohol Dependence: A Coping Skills Training Guide*. New York, NY: Guilford Press; 2002.

Müller KW, Janikian M, Dreier M, et al. Regular gaming behavior and Internet gaming disorder in European adolescents: results from a cross-national representative survey of prevalence, predictors, and psychopathological correlates. *Eur Child Adolesc Psychiatry*. 2015;24(5):565–574.

Nielsen Report. 2011. http://www.qj.net/wii/news/nielsen-59-us-households-have-wiis.html.

Olson CK, Kutner LA, Warner DE, Almerigi JB, Baer L, Nicholi AM, Beresin EV. Factors correlated with violent video game use by adolescent boys and girls. *J Adolesc Health.* 2007;41(1):77–83.

Pápay O, Urbán R, Griffiths MD, Nagygyörgy K, Farkas J, Kökönyei G, Felvinczi K, Oláh A, Elekes Z, Demetrovics Z. Psychometric properties of the problematic online gaming questionnaire short-form and prevalence of problematic online gaming in a national sample of adolescents. *Cyberpsychol Behav Soc Netw.* 2013;16(5):340–348.

Petry NM. *Pathological Gambling: Etiology, Comorbidity and Treatment.* Washington, DC: American Psychological Association Press; 2005.

Petry NM, Alessi SM, Byrne S, White WB. Reinforcing adherence to antihypertensive medications. *J Clin Hypertens.* 2015a;17(1):33–38.

Petry NM, Alessi SM, Rash CJ. A randomized study of contingency management in cocaine-dependent patients with severe and persistent mental health disorders. *Drug Alcohol Depend.* 2013a;130(1-3):234–237.

Petry NM, Andrade LF, Barry D, Byrne S. A randomized study of reinforcing ambulatory exercise in older adults. *Psychol Aging.* 2013b;28(4):1164–1173.

Petry NM, Barry D, Pescatello L, White WB. A low-cost reinforcement procedure improves short-term weight loss outcomes. *Am J Med.* 2011;124(11):1082–1085.

Petry NM, Rehbein F, Gentile DA, Lemmens JS, Rumpf HJ, Mößle T, Bischof G, Tao R, Fung DS, Borges G, Auriacombe M, González Ibáñez A, Tam P, O'Brien CP. An international consensus for assessing Internet gaming disorder using the new DSM-5 approach. *Addiction.* 2014;109(9):1399–1406.

Petry NM, Rehbein F, Ko CH, O'Brien CP. Internet gaming disorder in the DSM-5. *Curr Psychiatry Rep.* 2015b;17(9):72.

Piaget J. *Play, Dreams and Imitation.* New York, NY: Norton; 1962.

Plow M, Finlayson M. Potential benefits of Nintendo Wii fit among people with multiple sclerosis: A longitudinal pilot study. *Int J MS Care.* 2011;13(1):21–30.

Porter G, Starcevic V, Berle D, Fenech P. Recognizing problem video game use. *Aust N Z J Psychiatry.* 2010;44(2):120–128.

Przybylski AK. Electronic gaming and psychosocial adjustment. *Pediatrics.* 2014;134(3):e716–722.

Rehbein F, Kleimann M, Mössle T. Prevalence and risk factors of video game dependency in adolescence: results of a German nationwide survey. *Cyberpsychol Behav Soc Netw.* 2010;13:269–277.

Rehbein F, Kliem S, Baier D, Mößle T, Petry NM. Prevalence of Internet gaming disorder in German adolescents: diagnostic contribution of the

nine DSM-5 criteria in a statewide representative sample. *Addiction.*
2015;110:84251.

Rideout V. *Generation M2: Media in the Lives of 8- to 18-Year-Olds.* Menlo Park,
CA: Kaiser Family Foundation; 2010.

Roberts DF, Foehr UG. Trends in media use. *Future Child.* 2008;18(1):11–37.

Romer D, Bagdasarov Z, More E. Older versus newer media and the well-
being of United States youth: results from a national longitudinal panel. *J
Adolesc Health.* 2013;52(5):613–619.

Roozen HG, Boulogne JJ, van Tulder MW, van den Brink W, De Jong CA,
Kerkhof AJ. A systematic review of the effectiveness of the community
reinforcement approach in alcohol, cocaine and opioid addiction. *Drug
Alcohol Depend.* 2004;74:1–13.

Salguero RAT, Morán RMB. Measuring problem video game playing in
adolescents. *Addiction.* 2002;97(12):1601–1606.

Salmon A. Jail for couple whose baby died while they raised online child.
http://edition.cnn.com/2010/WORLD/asiapcf/05/28/south.korea.
virtual.baby/

Scharkow M, Festl R, Quandt T. Longitudinal patterns of problematic computer game use among adolescents and adults—a 2-year panel study.
Addiction. 2014;109(11):1910–1917.

Shaffer HJ, Hall MN, Vander Bilt J. Estimating the prevalence of disordered
gambling behavior in the United States and Canada: a research synthesis.
Am J Public Health. 1999;89:1369–1376.

Simons M, Bernaards C, Slinger J. Active gaming in Dutch adolescents: a de-
scriptive study. *Int J Behav Nutr Phys Act.* 2012;9:118.

Slutske WS. Natural recovery and treatment-seeking in pathological gambling:
results of two U.S. national surveys. *Am J Psychiatry.* 2006;163:297–302.

Slutske WS, Jackson KM, Sher KJ. The natural history of problem gambling
from age 18 to 29. *J Abnorm Psychol.* 2003;112(2):263–274.

Smith LJ, Gradisar M, King DL. Parental influences on adolescent video
game play: a study of accessibility, rules, limit setting, monitoring, and
cybersafety. *Cyberpsychol Behav Soc Netw.* 2015;18(5):273–279.

Smyth JM. Beyond self-selection in video game play: an experimental exami-
nation of the consequences of massively multiplayer online role-playing
game play. *Cyberpsychol Behav.* 2007;10(5):717–721.

Spragg A. 11 people who died playing video games. http://www.ranker.com/
list/8-people-who-died-playing-video-games/autumn-spragg.

Stanger C, Ryan SR, Scherer EA, Norton GE, Budney AJ. Clinic- and home-based contingency management plus parent training for adolescent cannabis use disorders. *J Am Acad Child Adolesc Psychiatry.* 2015;54(6):445–453.

Strong DR, Kahler CW. Evaluation of the continuum of gambling problems using the DSM-IV. *Addiction.* 2007;102(5):713–721.

Sun Y, Ying H, Seetohul RM, Xuemei W, Ya Z, Qian L, Guoqing X, Ye S. Brain fMRI study of crave induced by cue pictures in online game addicts. *Behav Brain Res.* 2012;233(2):563–576.

Swing EL, Gentile DA, Anderson CA, Walsh DA. Television and video game exposure and the development of attention problems. *Pediatrics.* 2010;126(2):214–221

Thomas NJ, Martin FH. Video-arcade game, computer game and Internet activities of Australian students: participation habits and prevalence of addiction. *Aust J Psychol.* 2010;62:59–66.

US Census. 2013; http://www.census.gov/hhes/computer/.

van Rooij AJ, Kuss DJ, Griffiths MD, Shorter GW, Schoenmakers MT, Van de Mheen D. The (co-)occurrence of problematic video gaming, substance use, and psychosocial problems in adolescents. *J Behav Addict.* 2014;3(3):157–165.

van Rooij AJ, Schoenmakers TM, van den Eijnden RJ, van de Mheen D. Compulsive Internet use: the role of online gaming and other internet applications. *J Adolesc Health.* 2010;47(1):51–57.

van Rooij AJ, Schoenmakers TM, Vermulst AA, van den Eijnden RJ, van de Mheen D. Online video game addiction: identification of addicted adolescent gamers. *Addiction.* 2011;106:205–212.

Volpp KG, John LK, Troxel AB, Norton L, Fassbender J, Loewenstein G. Financial incentive-based approaches for weight loss: a randomized trial. *JAMA.* 2008; 300(22):2631–2637.

Walther B, Morgenstern M, Hanewinkel R. Co-occurrence of addictive behaviours: personality factors related to substance use, gambling and computer gaming. *Eur Addict Res.* 2012;18(4):167–174.

Wittek CT, Finserås TR, Pallesen S, et al. Prevalence and predictors of video game addiction: a study based on a national representative sample of gamers. *Int J Ment Health Addict.* 2015: 1–15.

Winkler A, Dörsing B, Rief W, Shen Y, Glombiewski JA. Treatment of Internet addiction: a meta-analysis. *Clin Psychol Rev.* 2013;33(2):317–329.

Yee N. Motivations for play in online games. *Cyberpsychol Behav.* 2006; 9:772–775.

Young KS. Cognitive behavior therapy with Internet addicts: treatment outcomes and implications. *Cyberpsychol Behav.* 2007;10(5):671–679.

Zajac K, Ginley MK, Chang R, Petry NM. Treatments for Internet gaming disorder and Internet addiction: a systematic review. *Psychol Addict Behav.* 2017;31(8):979–994.

Index

Page references to tables and boxes are indicated by *t's* and *b's* respectively.